UP
THE
LADDER

UP THE LADDER

10 Essential Life Skills for Every Millennial to Fast-Track Their Career

Authored by

AKHIL IYER

Happy Self Publishing.

Contents

About the Author

Akhil, born on 19th August 1980 in New Delhi, completed his schooling from Somerville School Noida. As a kid, he bearhugged the dream to join the Indian Army. However, life had different plans for him and he became a Chartered Accountant. He completed his CA in the first attempt, achieving the 34th All India Rank at the age of 22.5 years. He is a Delhi University alumnus.

Securing 34th rank among tens of thousands and that too in the first attempt is like a feather in the cap. Anyone might speculate this boy might have got selected in the first interview and might have several options to choose from. If you are of the same opinion, let me startle you by revealing that Akhil got rejected by seven companies, one after another, before he landed in the job of a finance executive. Throughout his corporate journey, he learnt and implemented life skills to move **"Up The Ladder"** and went on to become an Assistant Director. During his 17-year professional journey, he worked with companies such as GE, American Express, Google, HSBC, British Council and Ernst Young.

Later he completed his Executive MBA from IIFT (Silver medallist), CIMA UK (Global Rank in E3), Diploma in IFRS and Green Belt in Quality.

He is an avid traveller and has visited 20 countries, mostly as part of his work. He loves writing and watching movies. He has been teaching the CIMA and ACCA students for 8 and 4+ years respectively. He had also been a guest faculty at Christ University (Bangalore) and Sikkim Manipal University (Jaipur).

Akhil often quotes – "***Till yesterday 'I Loved What I was Doing' and Today 'I am Doing What I Love'*** and he truly believes in it.

After a fulfilling corporate career of 17+ years, he decided to hang up his boots in April 2020 and started his second career-innings in his field of passion – Coaching and Mentoring professionals. He has mentored several young professionals in their pursuit of a "Great Career" in the corporate world.

Giving back to society has always been very close to his heart and to fulfil this dream, he co-founded **Hridaya Foundation** (an NGO) in 2012 with a Mission of

"Spreading Smile Every Mile". As part of this NGO, he set up a school with the purpose of "Bringing Education Closer to the underprivileged children". 150 bright and ambitious children study in this school. He received the **REX Karamveer Fellowship award** for his efforts in this field.

> *"Life should be a Collage of Experiences and not just an Accumulation of Wealth."*
> – **Akhil Iyer**

Through this book and his second career innings as a Coach and Mentor, he is on a **mission to support 500 Millennials in their career journey by the end of 2020 and 50k by the end of 2025.**

My Dear Beloved Mother
– Mrs. Manju Iyer (1956 – 2019)

This book is my tribute to my mother for being the great human she was and for the life she gave us (my sister and I) despite the infinite hardships.

Born in a very humble family, she completed her graduation in Chemistry (Hons) from Miranda College, Delhi University. After a brief corporate stint with a shipping company, she pursued the field of education.

She was a teacher both by profession and at heart. Geetanjali (my sister), several other students and I learnt the ropes of academics and most of the life skills from her. She was a great conversationalist and talking was her medicine for everything in life. She was a strong lady with an even stronger personality who never feared voicing her thoughts/opinions. With her contagious smile and a great sense of humour, she was one of the most loved people around. Resilience, Connecting the Dots, Being Humble, Learning from Failures, Discussing Things, all these are some of the essential life skills I learnt from her.

The biggest tragedy of my life happened on 19th July 2019, when my mother left us all for her heavenly abode. I can and will never come to terms with why God chose to take her away from us.

Mumma - You left us all very soon. Our biggest grudge for life is the fact that because you were so ill, Geetanjali and I could only communicate with you through sign language. I still feel very weak whenever I think of your 45-day battle against multiple illnesses and the last images of you. Not even a single day goes by when your absence is not felt.

Today what I am as an individual, I owe my life to you. It has only been possible because of your hard work, perseverance, sacrifices and vision about me and life.

I know it was one of your dreams to write a book. Writing this book is my humble effort to make your dream a reality. And there can be no better day than your birthday to release the book, 28th August.

I Miss You and Love You Mumma. I know you are around, watching and blessing me all the time. I wish and pray that you always shine like the brightest star.

Mumma stay Happy, Healthy and Live like a Princess wherever you are!!

Acknowledgements

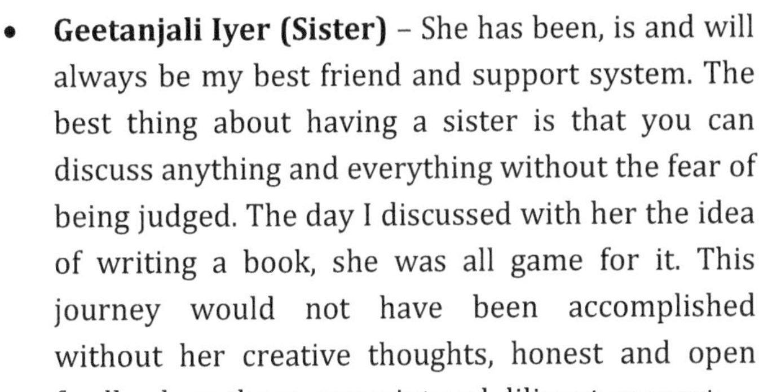

- **Geetanjali Iyer (Sister)** – She has been, is and will always be my best friend and support system. The best thing about having a sister is that you can discuss anything and everything without the fear of being judged. The day I discussed with her the idea of writing a book, she was all game for it. This journey would not have been accomplished without her creative thoughts, honest and open feedback on the manuscript and diligent support.

- **Nikhil Khullar (Brother-in-Law)** – He is a very open-minded person and believes in not only trying out new things but also encourages others to do so. He was very supportive when I wanted to switch tracks and follow my passion. "It might take time to settle down but it is worth a genuine try," these were his words that boosted my confidence

- **Jyotsana Ramchandran (Author-Coach)** – My coach and guide in my pursuit to write my first book. I had seen a lot of advertisements on Facebook of different people who were running different courses on writing a book. The reason I decided to enrol myself with Author Success Academy was only because of Jyotsana. She came across as a positive and humble person willing to help other people achieve their dream of becoming an author.

- **Sushmitha (A friend)** - An energetic and highly customer-centric employee cum brand ambassador of Happy Self Publishing. She and her team managed my book project with the utmost professionalism. It would not have been possible without her.

- **Nitin** - A friend who is fortunately also a very thorough and impeccable editor. He played an important role in reading my entire manuscript as a critical reader and shared suggestions for improvement. Thank you, Nitin, for being a part of this journey.

- **Ratna Dhar Mam (Teacher & Guru from School)** – One of my favourite teachers from Somerville School. The school and her efforts have played a vital role in whoever I am today. She is a happy-go-lucky person who is always passionate to help students and children. She is blessed with the gift of the gab. Her energy levels are infectious and in school, all I needed was a pep talk with her to get back on track.

- **Promila Mehta Mam (Teacher & Guru from School)** – Even while being a teacher she was a friend to me. One of the most liked teachers in the Somerville school. She taught us mathematics and I guess it was because of my mother and Promila Mam's efforts that I have become a CA today. Her contagious smile and positive attitude towards situations always instilled confidence to become better versions of ourselves.

- **Charu Mittal (Mentor)** – My first mentor in the corporate world. Thinking out of the box, problem-solving and building a high-performing team are traits that I learnt from her and made them an integral part of my career.

- **Kshama Dhir (Mentor)** – It started with just a "Hi" in GECIS and later led to working directly with her in EY (Ernst & Young). We share common interests in the field of education, corporate social responsibility and travel. Sharp business acumen and connecting the dots are the life skills that I learnt from her in my corporate career.

- **Archana Chettiar (Fellow Author and Content Developer)** – She has been my accountability partner throughout the journey of this book. This book would not have transformed into black and white without the active inputs and support from her.

- **Hiral Dhruv (Creative Designer)** – A creative person at heart. She designed the cover for my book and is a good friend now.

- **Dr. Major Rupinder Kaur (Friend and Business Partner)** – A friend and guide whom I met through LinkedIn. We share a similar passion to support young professionals in building great careers.

- **Anuj Jagannathan (Friend)** – An old friend who is highly energetic and loves to follow his passion. An author at heart who not only shared his experience of writing the book but also guided me throughout my journey.

- Other people who have helped and guided me through the journey of writing this book are -
  - **Radha Abrol (Mentor)** – Managing Director at Accenture
  - **Christoph Steinlen (Guide)** – Partner at Ernst & Young Germany
  - **Aseem Bajaj (1st Counsellor)** - Tax Director at Smith & Nephew Plc.
  - **Veena Sinha (Guide)** - Head of Information Services, Culture Change & Corporate Wellness

CHAPTER I

Life may not give 2 chances — You need to give yourself 2 or more plans instead

I was an average student but I also believed in working to improve myself. In the 10th standard, I secured 85% marks. I wanted to improve my score in the 12th standard. The reason behind it is well-known. I think, for my 12th standard, I prepared well and my exams also went well. But when the results were announced, my thinking was proved wrong. I secured 78% which not only failed to meet my expectations but also broke my dream of seeking admission in my favourite colleges in Delhi University.

Relatives from my maternal side were mostly engineers and/or related to the medical profession. On the other hand, relatives from my paternal side were either in marketing or business. None of which fascinated me. Instead, I chose commerce as per my understanding. Career options that I later had were CA, CS and ICWA. I am sure there would have been other career options as well but somehow, I lacked the motivation to do a self-research. Social media platforms like LinkedIn, Facebook, etc. wherein I could post a question and professionals could overwhelm me with suggestions and ideas, did not exist. I thought of getting some guidance from known people with a commerce background. After all, getting relevant industry knowledge could make a difference.

After inquiring with a few friends, I was referred to a contact. I was directed to Mr. Kumar who presumably had a good experience in the field of finance and accounting. I booked an appointment with him and went to meet him at his residence along with my mom.

Me – *Hello Uncle, how are you doing?*

Mr. Kumar – *Son I am doing very well. How can I help you?*

Me – *Uncle I wanted to discuss with you the opportunities that I can pursue in the field of finance and accounting given that I have now completed my 12th standard.*

Mr. Kumar – *How many marks have you scored?*

Me – *Uncle my best of 4 is 80%.*

Mr. Kumar – *This is very less. I am afraid that you may not get admission in the top colleges in Delhi University.*

Wow! Those were like very motivating words. I would have been very naïve in life but one thing that I understood was that when someone comes to seek guidance, it is essential to make the person comfortable and also make an attempt to motivate the person. Mr. Kumar was far from either of these. I doubted whether I had been referred to the right person and if by the end of this conversation, will I be able to get the right direction. We continued with the conversation.

Mr. Kumar – *Son, let me say this – there are limited options to build a career in finance and accounting. The best option I can think of for you is to pursue Chartered Accountancy. It would take you a minimum of 4.5 years to complete. While the passing percentage is less but job prospects post completion are good.*

At least he narrowed down the options from CA, CS and ICWA to just CA, which was now a sign of relief and that gave me some confidence in Mr. Kumar.

Me – *Uncle, isn't doing graduation compulsory. Isn't that true?*

This might sound stupid, but I tried asking the questions that were there in my head. As it is said, "The only stupid questions are the questions that are never asked", so I did not hesitate to ask.

Mr. Kumar – *I have suggested a professional course. If you complete your CA, there is no need for you to do graduation separately. After you become a CA, no one would even ask you about your graduation.*

For the first time, while having a conversation with him, I felt good. He was indicating that I didn't have to bother doing both B. Com (Hons) and then CA. That was such a big relief.

Me – *Uncle as you said that the passing percentage of CA is very less. Now, if I take more than the usual time to complete my CA, then what would be my job prospects?*

Mr. Kumar – *You are thinking way too far. For now, enrol yourself into the course and start doing it. The question of a job will arise much later.*

Me – *Would you be able to recommend me to any CA whom I can talk to? This will help me get more clarity.*

Mr. Kumar – *Son, don't waste time talking to too many people. Just start the course.*

Me – *Uncle I just want to be double-sure that I should not go for graduation along with CA.*

Mr. Kumar – *Son, have you ever seen a person going for a boat ride in two boats at the same time?*

Me – *No, that is not possible and does not even sound practical.*

Me – *Thank you, uncle, for talking to me and providing me guidance.*

I knew he was doing me a favour by answering my questions. So, I refrained from asking any further questions as from his tone, he sounded a little irritated with my questions which made me feel uncomfortable. When we were in school, we knew that after pre-nursery would be schooling. 1st standard would be followed by 2nd standard class and so on. There was a specific curriculum to follow. However, after the 10th standard, we have to make the important decision of choosing a stream (Commerce, Science or Humanity). After 12th standard comes another milestone of life and that is the decision that would define our professional journey.

While mom and I were walking back home, I told her that I was relieved, as I would not have to burden myself by doing 2 courses at the same time. All mothers are God-gifted in terms of logic and practicality and my mother always used this to perfection. She knew that it was maybe not the right time for any further conversation as I was under the direct influence of the thoughts shared by Mr. Kumar.

We reached home. To detach me from overthinking, she reminded me that it was time to go and play cricket. Just when I was ready to go, I looked back, mom smiled and said - Enjoy the game and we would continue the discussion later in the evening.

That day, I just could not focus on my match and halfway through, I came back home to continue the discussion. I felt as if I had grown up, as I was getting serious about my career and life ahead. I felt my career was more important than a game of cricket. While noticing my bamboozled expressions, mom asked me what I had thought based on the nuggets that I got from Mr. Kumar.

Since I was unclear, I proposed to do my research on the topic basis which I would come back to her with my thoughts. My mother being a practical person, never enforced her decision or thoughts on me. Rather she wanted to inculcate the decision-making ability in me and owning them completely. It was like, you would take a horse to drink water once or twice and then you would want the horse to find water himself.

I went to an internet café to gather more details about CA. The research was surely interesting and helped me in developing a better understanding of what I was getting into. I read about the CA exam pattern, the timing of the exams and preconditions to apply. One of the good things that I understood about CA was about their Articleship program which I thought would also make me job-ready. I compared the CA and B. Com (H) curriculum and understood that there were a lot of commonalities. That was a definite confidence-booster.

I went back home, sat down to share and discuss my findings with mom. We agreed that I would enrol myself for B. Com (Hons) and simultaneously prepare for CA. Even if I took more than the expected time in completing CA, I would at least be a graduate after 3 years. Mom gave me a lot of comfort by reiterating that I should not pursue CA with some pressure in my mind. I felt comfortable, confident and relaxed as the important decision-making process was completed.

I started my B. Com (Hons) and CA journey in 1998. In 2001, I completed my graduation and by November 2002, I also completed my CA. A big personal achievement for me was that I completed both the courses within the minimum time possible.

During this entire process, I learnt an important life skill.

After I started my corporate journey, I got the opportunity to work in different roles and learn new things. After working for almost 8 years, I started to tire out due to the excessively demanding corporate life. While I was doing well, I started thinking about a plan B for my career as well. Whatever the plan would be, I presumed that I would need time to think, plan and execute it. Trust me, there is no right time to do things in life, but whenever you get an idea, my advice is to take the thought seriously. You learn by doing, you get more clarity by being in the action-mode and most importantly, you understand the sustainability of your interest in that area.

My Plan A was to continue with my corporate life and Plan B was to be in the student community. I wanted to teach students, nurture young professionals and be a coach and mentor to them in the domain of their career. As I share this with you, I realise that the aspiration to become a coach has come from my mother. While I continued with my corporate career, I started investing my time, energy and money in preparing for my future alternative career as well. Any profession that you choose would need you to build two things – (1) Your Brand and (2) Your Credibility.

While I continued with my primary job from Monday to Friday, I started investing my weekends for my alternative career. Candidly, I started to enjoy it even more. After a hectic corporate week, I used to eagerly wait for the weekend. I started working on my 2nd career plan in 2012. After a fulfilling career of working for some of the corporate giants, I decided to take the bold step to embark on a journey of becoming a full-time Coach and Mentor in 2020.

All the professionals I interact with as a mentor/coach, my advice to them is to always have Plan A and B. I help them think about different plans, evaluate them, research them and understand the pros and cons. The plan could be related to their work, career, education, etc. Most importantly, every professional/individual needs to take complete ownership of their plans. Once the planning is done, they should start to engage themselves in active experimentation. Only when we start working on some of our ideas, do we understand the real challenges as well as the sustainability of our interest in that specific area. After trying a few things, I have realised that reality is different from what we generally think it would be.

Lessons Learnt

- Take inputs from others but do not rely on them blindly.
- Self-research is very important. It not only clears a lot of doubts that you may have but also empowers you to take complete ownership of the task that you have signed up for.
- Always have a plan A and B right at the start. In some cases, you may need a Plan C as well.
- There is always a thin line between Confidence and Over Confidence.
- Benjamin Franklin said, **"Failing to Plan is like Planning to Fail"**. So, after you have inked a plan, you must get some hands-on experience to litmus-test if this is what you actually want.

CHAPTER 2

Connecting the Dots

Vishal, I am delighted to share with you that as part of this year's performance management process, the leadership team is very happy with your performance. Your rating is –

Goals – 1 (on a scale of 1-5 wherein "1" is the best and "5" is the worst)

Leadership – 1 (on a scale of 1-5 wherein "1" is the best and "5" is the worst)

Vishal was delighted to hear the news and thanked the company, leadership and me for all the support and guidance during his journey. He was one of the three senior analysts in my team.

The reason we were having this conversation was because of an earlier discussion that I had with all my senior analysts at the beginning of the year when we met for the goal-setting activity. Based on our understanding of the team/departmental goals, we chalked out our individual goals and ensured that they added up as well. We also ensured that goals were motivating for all the team members to make the extra effort to achieve them.

Vishal was inquisitive and believed in understanding the microscopic details of things that he would sign up to deliver. After the meeting, he approached me for a follow-up discussion over the next few days. While everyone else would have immediately got busy working on their goals, Vishal took a step back to understand and plan things better before beginning to execute. This quality differentiated Vishal from his peers. Despite being new, he had become an integral part of the team with his diligent approach to plan and execute things.

I was working in a shared service centre and our team was responsible for performing the month-end accounting tasks. These activities generally lasted for 10-12 working days and there was always the added pressure of meeting stringent timeliness. From a different perspective, these were also the days which were the best days to test the team members and observe their behaviour in difficult and stressful situations.

Amit and Sachin were the other two senior analysts in my team. The tasks of our team were so critical that even if Diwali was on a weekday, we had to be in the office. In the year 2005, Diwali was on a weekday. That was a typical situation as most of the critical activities were due to be executed on that day. Compared to the other months, we had 2-3 hours less to complete the same set of activities. However, the team was confident that they would be able to manage the situation.

As the leader of the team, I wanted to use this opportunity to take a calculated risk and test the succession planning that I had worked on with my senior analysts (Future leaders). True leaders rise to the occasion in difficult times and this was a perfect time for Vishal, Amit and Sachin to display their leadership potential.

Each of my senior analysts worked according to a particular approach.

Sachin and his approach

He was a happy-go-lucky kind of person. He preferred a directive style of leadership and would follow instructions only in black and white. He seemed overconfident as he did not see any challenge in the situation. He took it as a regular month. With his style of working, I observed that he lacked a sense of urgency to complete the tasks. Therefore, he did not spend the extra time to support and review the work of some of the new joiners in the team. His only priority was to complete all his tasks accurately and within the overall time that we had as a team. His personal performance was also his benchmark.

Interestingly, he was least interested in taking additional tasks/responsibilities as a senior member of the team and despite this attitude, he aspired for vertical growth. Despite low acceptance in the team and repeated feedback, he did not take things seriously. I decided to take a calculated risk. Only for the current month, I swapped his regular activities with those on which he had been cross-trained a couple of months back. Sachin was perplexed and felt that was being done on purpose.

Unfortunately, the new joiners in the team could not pick the complex tasks and as a leader of the team, I could not let them be exposed. That was time for senior members like Sachin to step up and take charge. **Connecting the dots** in this situation, I had a back-up plan ready. In case Sachin would face any challenge in completing the tasks, I would personally do them. This was exactly what happened and when Sachin walked up to me for help, I did the needful. The situation was an eye-opener for Sachin. The next day he came and said that he realised he had been in his comfort zone and there was a serious need for him to adapt. He thanked me for helping him and prevented a disaster from happening.

Sachin confided that earlier there were times when he purposefully did not help other people so that he could continue to enjoy the uninterrupted mileage and importance within the team. This was unfortunately his **"Survival of the fittest strategy"** and it seemed to be working for him till last year with his previous team leader. Towards the end of the conversation, he said –

- "I wish I had worked on the areas of improvement that you had highlighted and also how they would benefit me and the team". Sachin always got the best rating when it came to goals but leadership was always his weak area. He also understood that his perception about the organisation not promoting him purposely was incorrect.
- He thanked me for teaching him a life skill which would be relevant in both his professional and personal life.

Amit and his approach

He knew about the tasks that he had to perform and banked on his efficiency in completing them. Despite the shorter time window, he was confident about completing all his tasks and volunteered to help the new joiners. After reaching office, without wasting any time, he immediately started working. While executing his tasks, he realised that there was an issue in the source data and he would need to re-do the entire process.

Amit was generally a calm person but this time, he started panicking especially due to the fear of missing the timeliness. While he had a good network within the organisation, everyone he reached out to was busy with their work and could not offer him instant support to his problem. He reached out to me and requested my intervention. I understood the situation and reached out to senior people in other teams to check if other people from their team could expedite the tasks on which Amit was dependant. Finally, things started moving and Amit looked relieved. He also got support from Vishal. In the interim, he started helping other members of the team if they were getting stuck anywhere.

At this moment, I got the wind of another key element – Teaming can be best taught on the job. The team had a very different aura that day – maybe it was just Diwali and I was over-reading the situation. ☺

Amit realised 2 things while working during the current month

- When we continue to do the same work, we can become complacent and there is a high possibility that we also stop thinking out of the box. He surely missed **"Connecting the Dots"** - The timeliness had not only reduced for our team but for the other teams also who were involved in the process. He missed out on discussing and planning things with the other teams. Discussions always give a different perspective and asking for help should not be interpreted as a comparative of your capability vs. someone else's.

- No matter how smooth things look, there can be surprises. We need to plan for contingencies both in our personal and professional lives.

Vishal and his approach

Vishal had his set of activities and supported the European region. That was a peculiar month as we had 2-3 hours less as compared to all previous months. That was the most important element and amongst the 3 senior analysts, it was Sachin who took it the most seriously. Given that the task had extra significance, he deliberated more on this to plan his work better.

He was proactive in his approach and always believed in breaking down the larger task to smaller ones and then spend time in **"Connecting the dots"**. For every activity that he had a dependency on, he connected with every individual/team in person. He wanted to understand their plan of execution and clarify (in advance) if there were any disconnects.

Given the shorter timelines, he reviewed the data that he had received in advance and raised queries with concerned people. He also replicated the previous month's templates so that he could get data on time and initiate his work.

His methodical and proactive approach based on the aspect of **"Connecting the Dots"** ensured that he completed all his tasks seamlessly and before time. He utilized the time that he saved to help Amit in completing his tasks.

After the month-end, my peers from the Asia Pacific team told me that Vishal had reached out to them well before Diwali to understand the best practices which enabled them to complete tasks in a shorter time window. He used the learning's to complete his work. He volunteered to conduct training for members of my team to share these best practices.

Based on how Vishal supported the team, other members of the team nominated him for a reward. In fact, I still remember a few team members personally giving him "Thank You" cards for his help. Vishal had truly risen to the occasion and demonstrated leadership qualities. He was a person who never had any insecurity in sharing his learnings with the team.

His topmost priority was to ensure that the team was able to complete the tasks and achieve the goals.

The list of appreciations for Vishal was still not over and it seemed that it was his golden month. We received a note from our stakeholder appreciating the efforts put in by the team especially during the Diwali week. The email had a special note of thanks for Vishal. While **"Connecting the Dots"** he even kept his offshore counterparts in the loop to ensure better coordination and resolution of issues, if any, as a part of the closure process.

My peers and I (from different fields), in a career spanning two decades, have observed and discussed the importance of the skill - **"Connecting the Dots"**. We recommend it as a must-have key skill that every millennial should have in their armoury.

Lessons Learnt

"Connecting the Dots" is a key skill that:

- Differentiates a star performer from a good performer.
- A good leader demonstrates at all times.
- Enables you to see the complete picture and understand the nuisances before attempting to solve the issue or leverage an opportunity.
- Practicing this skill continuously strengthens your problem-solving ability also.
- Every professional who can ideate and innovate has an innate ability of **"Connecting the Dots"** all the time and every time.

CHAPTER 3

Celebrating Failure

Tring Tring.... Tring, Tring.... My all-time sturdy Nokia 3310 rang. It was my friend – Mukesh. We used to live in the same area and meet almost every day. However, this time, we were meeting after a few months and the common reason that we both had for not being able to catch up was that we were busy in our corporate jobs and other priorities of life. ☺

I informed my mom and went downstairs to meet him. I saw him waiting in his car which was a sign that he had not come for a quick chat. We drove to one of our favourite market places which have several eating-joint options. Despite meeting after a long time, our instant topic of discussion was our corporate life. It seemed that we were both feeling directionless. It is ironic that when we are in school, we crave to live our college life. After reaching college, the corporate world becomes our fantasy land. And now we realise that school life was the best.

I would rather say we Humans are quite fanciful; we are curious beings. We keep wanting more and when we get it, either it is not worth or our desire for something more robs our moment of current happiness.

So, coming back to the meeting with Mukesh, while talking, cribbing and playing our favourite songs, we reached the market. We parked the car and began our search for a good, relatively peaceful place to sit and talk. We chose a South Indian restaurant. The moment we placed our order, we were joined by a few other common friends.

Hey, hi, how are things and what's Happening – The slang started. I realised that it would be a long night as there are very rare moments nowadays when the timings match to meet each other. I called up mom and urged her to sleep and eat on time. Majorly, like all mothers, she would get concerned if I was not back at home by a certain time (in my case it was 10 PM). So, she asked me to come home on time. I smiled while resting the phone on the table as our definition of time was implicitly different. While everyone shared the latest that was happening in their lives, surprisingly everyone just had their corporate lives to discuss and talk about. Even after the dinner was over, we felt there was so much still left to chin-wag about. So, one of the friends got up and suggested to drive down to a little far off place which sold stuffed bread (The Great Indian Naan). Were we still hungry? No! But we always have some mysterious space in our stomach that is always empty and is ready to taste some new food.

After driving for an hour and a half, we reached the place. Since it was a long drive, some more space got created in our stomach. We again ordered food and the corporate chit-chat continued.

The owner of the restaurant, who happened to overhear our conversations, came to check with us if everything was fine. We responded affirmatively. He introduced himself as Mr. Khanna. He said, "I was listening to your talks and it appears that a lot of things are not going right." Our instant response was, "Yes you are Right. Life at this moment is a bit challenging and the least we can do is sit, vent out and learn from each other." Mr. Khanna smiled and continued in his husky voice "I have had a lot of failures in my life. I have trodden through more downs than ups. However, whenever I felt things were not going as per plans, you know what I did?" His question was for all of us. Given that he would not have done what we were doing (complaining about almost everything), we kept quiet.

Mr. Khanna said, "**Whenever I used to fail, I used to celebrate.**" We all looked at each other, as if saying – Dude this cannot be true. How can you celebrate when you have failed? He further went on saying, "By celebrating success, I know I am learning, that I have the appetite to take the risk and I am just not willing to give up." The way he said it left a strong impression on me.

He went back to work, but his pep-talk left me in a pool of intense thoughts. At that moment, I was physically present with friends but I felt Mr. Khanna's words resonating in my mind. I have always been a wanderer. After excusing myself from the group, I went for a stroll. I remembered the days when I was a kid and had this fascination to learn how to ride a bicycle. I cannot even count the number of times I would have fallen and hurt myself. But it never lowered my morale and giving up was never a choice. After days of practicing, I finally became a pro at riding it. I am sure if you also know how to ride a bike, then you would also have gone through a similar journey. So, being engrossed in my thoughts, as I looked back, I realised I had covered some distance.

I came back. We bid goodnight to each other and hoped to meet soon. Mukesh and I went back in his car. As we drove back home, I spoke to Mukesh about what Mr. Khanna shared. As kids, that was what we exactly used to do. We unknowingly celebrated success. During the journey of this fast-paced life, we easily get disheartened, demotivated and have forgotten to

"Celebrate Failure". Mukesh agreed and we promised ourselves to reinstate this learning in our lives.

It has been more than a decade since this incident happened but the learning has been forever.

"Even when you are sure of falling, continue to take small steps. Only your steps will take you to your destination." – Akhil Iyer

I bet you, find me a single person (amongst the 7.8 billion human beings) who has not had any failure in his/her life. I have had so many failures in my life that I have made failure my best friend and I call him Mr. F. This Mr. F is always around me. There is no field in which I have not had a selfie with Mr. F. I guess, we both look good together in the frame of life. I have failed in

- Exams
- Sports
- Business when I along with my colleagues started a food venture
- Interviews
- Situations wherein I have let myself down
- Relationships

The list is just endless. Every failure has given me learning for the rest of my life. Mr. F never leaves me alone but he now knows that I have whatever it takes to overpower him. Many professionals whom I meet, barricade themselves from doing things because they fear failure. More than the journey or the experiences, we tend to think about the outcome. **Metaphorically** if the glass is half empty, it is also half full at the same time.

In one of the professional exams that I had appeared for, despite my good preparations, I failed. I could only attempt a 90-mark paper and thus I transferred the onus of failing to that one 10-mark question which I left. I did not take failure to my heart and decided to re-appear. In my second attempt, even though I attempted all the questions, I failed again. I did not want to be naïve again and find another excuse. I accepted my failure and decided to self-reflect. I realised that I needed to prepare myself even more discreetly. This time, I started to look at some of the past papers and suggested answers. As I went through the past papers and read answers written by the invigilators, I saw a clear gap in the approach I was following. While my approach was the traditional **rote** approach, the invigilator was more focussed on an application-oriented, problem-solving approach. I called a friend who had also failed, to share my learnings and to pep him up. He said– **You seem to be happy that you have failed.** He was right, not just in my voice but also in terms of my actions, I wanted to celebrate. I wanted to celebrate the understanding that I had developed about the approach to clear my exam. Disheartened, my friend decided not to appear for the exams any further. I went and gave my attempt number 3. This time, I passed. I was elated.

Stephen Covey has rightly talked about the 90/10 principle. 10% of what happens to us in our life is "Destiny" and 90% is based on "how we react" to the 10%.

I have learnt that there are 2 types of failures:

- When you give up without trying
- When you try, don't succeed and you give up

Think through again. When you try and do not succeed, the general tendency is to think that you have failed. However, take this failure as learning for your next opportunity.

DO NOT overburden yourself with the pressure of succeeding every time and all the time. While it is a great attitude to walk with, it is even more important to enjoy the journey and the process.

"Celebrate failure as it gives you the courage to aim for even greater success in life."

Lessons Learnt

- There is always a reason why you are still a step/few steps away from succeeding.
- Self-reflection and a better understanding of the situation will always help you find solutions to overcome the challenges.
- Embrace and celebrate failure. Cherish the learnings from it.
- Pick a couple of situations from your personal/professional life and evaluate the reasons neutrally. I bet you would now realise what you could have done differently or maybe you are already doing it. Make this a habit, it works
- Succeeding after failing is necessary for your betterment. Never do it to prove a point to people around you.
- Look around you; every single person has failed at least once in life so far.
- We all love to watch stories of other people depicting their failures and how they bounced back. But our failure stories are like nightmares to us.

CHAPTER 4

Challenge the status quo – It will be your gateway to newer and bigger opportunities

About 10-11 people were sitting in a conference and the topic of discussion was a process that had to be transitioned from the US to India. Eva (The program sponsor) and Michael (Project Owner) had come to India with their contingent to discuss and decide. Team leads who had transitioned similar processes in the past were present to share their experiences and suggestions. I was new to the entire setup and in fact, it was my first experience of working in an MNC. While the discussions were happening, I was busy doing 2 things:

- I was taking notes for my understanding and future reference
- I kept my eyes and ears open and this helped me put things in perspective

Overall, the meetings and discussions were planned for over 3 days. 7-8 different teams were expected to present their best cases over the 3-day period. I had spent a lot of time and energy to put in place an overall plan and coordinate with the teams. I consolidated the presentations and also tabulated other logistics (calendar invites, booking conference rooms, etc.)

Day 1 started with greetings, introductions, purpose, approach and the outcome expected by the end of day 3. Eva and Michael shared an update about their office, team and the work they were doing. Post lunch, team leaders representing different teams started their presentation one by one. By the end of day 1, we managed to cover 3 teams. Based on the discussions, I had a few thoughts running in my mind which were different from what was generally being proposed and discussed so far. I had always been conditioned to wait for my turn to be asked for my inputs.

Day 2 also had back-to-back meetings. There was a dinner planned for everybody to informally meet and catch up. I was restless to have a discussion with Eva about the idea that I had and hear her thoughts about it. During the dinner, while a colleague and I were generally chit-chatting, Eva came and stood beside us. She asked us – How do we feel about the discussions so far? I could not resist and shared my thoughts with her. After a brief discussion, we all started having dinner and finally, it was time to go back home.

Day 3 – We were all there in the conference room for the grand finale. Eva and Michael had to summarise the 2-day discussion and their plan with us. This could have been a big opportunity for all of us. They were looking to set up an 8-10-member team to transition the process over the next 6 months from the US to India. We were told that the person leading the team would be someone from the existing set of team leaders and I happened to be one of them. One thing that was running in my mind was the fact that I saw Eva talking to Siddharth (my manager) right before the meeting. I was worried if it was about the suggestions that I gave over dinner last night and if they were not even relevant. We all have this habit of speculating and I was no different.

Before Eva and Michael made the big announcement, they asked if anyone had any final point(s) to put onto the table. I took that as an opportunity to share my viewpoint and raised my hand. I said that while all approaches looked good, time would be an important element. I suggested if the project manager could travel to the US for 2-3 weeks to meet the stakeholders and gather the requirements. That would help in preparing better for all the other elements related to the transition such as hiring, training, IT setup, etc. That would make the transition smoother and give more time for both the teams to settle in. There was pin-drop silence after I finished talking. A few people (including Eva, Michael and Siddharth) gazed at me.

The reason I said what I said was due to an instance that happened 2 months back when I had joined that organisation. My Manager Siddharth took me for a coffee and briefed me about an upcoming meeting with Deepak (our AVP). We spent a lot of late nights putting together a 40-page presentation for a 3-hour review session. I got actively involved in preparing the presentation. It was crucial for me to obtain a deeper understanding of the work.

Deepak sat quietly, hearing Siddharth talk for almost 2.5 hours. During the presentation, I had some suggestions to give but was afraid to speak up as I was too new. After Siddharth ended the presentation, Deepak did not look very happy and said – You and your team are doing a lot of work. However, I feel that you all need to look at better ways of doing things. I felt bad as I had a few points that I wanted to talk about. I just wished and hoped "What if I had said what I wanted to; the meeting could have been different."

I understood the message and went to Siddharth, asking for his permission to lead the meeting with Eva in 2 months from then. He was okay with me leading the meeting despite being new.

Coming back to the 3-day meeting, Eva started sharing her inputs. She began by thanking everyone for the presentations and intense discussions over the last 2 days. She was happy to be in India and it turned out to be a good decision to have these discussions in person. She also said that it was good to see different teams presenting their best practices and challenging each other about the best way forward.

She approved the overall project plan for a team of 8 professionals to travel to the US for a period of 6 months and transition the process to India. Post completion of the transition, a majority of the process would be run from India with minimal support from members of her US team. There was applause and smiles all around the conference room.

The next step was to hear from her about the approach, how she wanted to begin the transition. She wanted to divide it into 2 phases -

Phase 1 – Project manager to travel to the US to meet the stakeholders and gather requirements. After returning to India, the project manager would hire a team and conduct basic level training. This would help the team settle well before they are finally ready to travel to the US. As a result of this, the acclimatization period after the team would reach the US, would also be shorter.

Phase 2 – The entire team to travel to the US for a period of 6 months for the on-job training. Post return to India, the team will have 2-3 months to stabilise the process and announce Go Live.

This was exactly the approach that I had recommended over our discussion at the dinner table on the previous night. I gave myself a virtual pat on the back; it was all due to my curiosity to challenge the status quo. There are always better and effective ways to do things. We need to think, find and discuss about them.

I was selected to lead the transition of the new process. Deepak was convinced of this approach. Rest is all history as they say. I went to meet the stakeholders as planned and on my return to India hired a team. Even before the team got their visas for further advanced training, we started supporting the team in the US. As a result, we were able to make good progress, demonstrate results and most importantly; build rapport.

Soon after we all got our visas; we went for a comprehensive training plan. The acclimatization period was relatively quick and the rapport was built on a strong foundation.

We completed the training successfully and started managing the entire process from India. The team in the US focussed on expanding the business.

Job after Job, I held on to the aspect of **"Challenging the Status Quo"** for the benefit of the organisation, team and also for myself. I continued to expand my horizon and this helped me in my pursuit of growth.

> *"Know where you want to go and make sure the right people know about it."*
> *– Meredith Mahoney*

The next big break

In one of my future jobs, I was called by John – he was one of my hiring managers. We met over lunch and during that conversation, he directed me to David who wanted some help with an accounting concept. Being a Chartered Accountant, I thought it would be easy and I gladly accepted to meet him. He was one of the stakeholders for a critical project which involved multiple companies, countries and teams.

David found my advice helpful. While talking to him, I realised that other members of the project were also focussed on only their part of the project. Working in silos would not help and there was a need to bring them all together on the same page. Big or small, new or old all companies have this task to encourage people to come out of silo working and get into collaborative ways of working.

In the current situation also, it seemed that none of the stakeholders were communicating with each other. I went up to John and told him about my interaction with David. I sought his permission to meet the project manager (Sachin). I had a few things in mind that I wanted to share with him. John immediately agreed and I scheduled a time to meet Sachin.

Sachin and I met and introduced ourselves briefly. I mentioned to Sachin about the conversation with David and told him that there were 2 other people whom I thought were key to the project and thus it was important to interact with them. Sachin agreed at that very moment. While engaging with the two people, I realised that it was important to bring all the stakeholders on a single platform. I went to Sachin and shared my plan with him. He calibrated on it for some time and asked me to set up a meeting to interact with all the stakeholders in a week from then. I was happy and felt that I was adding value to the project already.

After sending the meeting invite, I started interacting with the stakeholders to build rapport with them. Before the date of the meeting, I met all of them and gathered inputs. I consolidated them for the presentation at the meeting. I was doing all this out of my own curiosity, learning and most importantly, challenging the status quo in which things were/would be done. Based on everyone's inputs, I put together the following things:

- An end-to-end process flow diagram
- Roles and responsibilities of all the stakeholders with respect to the project
- An overall project plan
- A list of the next steps

Finally, the day came and I was slightly nervous. It could turn out to be a big day if everything went well. I had run the presentation past Sachin and had incorporated his inputs overnight. However, not just in India but elsewhere also people do not turn up for meetings on time. While we were waiting for others to join, people started their conversations and slowly the conference room sounded like a fish market. People in groups were having diverse conversations about the project. While I wanted to bring everyone's attention to the presentation, Sachin looked at me and gestured me to let people continue to talk.

I sat down and started to scroll up and down the presentation. While overhearing the stakeholder's conversation, I gathered that most of them were actually talking about the risks involved in the project. I had projected the list of challenges that I had gathered in my 1/1 conversations along with a mitigation plan for each of them. Two senior stakeholders called out my name and asked me to walk them through the challenges captured in the presentation. As a result, all other stakeholders also started looking at the presentation and there was peace in the room. One of them said, "We have all been talking about it but it seems you already have it for us. Let us look at them one by one." In my mind I said to myself, this is exactly what I said earlier, provided everyone paid attention.

Nonetheless, I finally went through the list of all challenges and there was now a healthy debate amongst the participants. We achieved the following objectives from the meeting:

- All stakeholders now knew each other by name
- All stakeholders were able to visualise and understand their role in the project more clearly
- They understood how their tasks were related to each other
- Agreements and disagreements were openly talked about and collectively we started reaching common solutions as well
- We established a weekly cadence of accountability

The meeting was scheduled for 2 hours. However, it spanned for almost 3 hours but still, no one complained. It seemed that everyone found value in the discussion. The best moment was when Steve (a senior stakeholder) spoke to Sachin and said, "This was a brilliant idea to get us all together on a common platform to discuss. I am glad that you and Akhil took this initiative." I am sure that all the participants truly appreciated the need to **"Challenge the Status Quo"**. We could have exchanged several emails related to the project but I guess the last 3 hours of exchanging dialects had given us so much clarity.

Steve further said, "We have discussed and covered most of the items in person and I see that everyone is committed to make this project a success." On behalf of everyone, he proposed if I (Akhil) could be nominated as the Deputy PMO to work alongside Sachin on the project. He asserted, "Akhil has already done the groundwork, everyone has spoken to him in person and we all value his efforts."

Sachin agreed to Steve's idea and looked at me for my consent. That was a big learning opportunity for me and I immediately responded with a Yes. We all shook hands and left the meeting room. Sachin called me to his office to acknowledged the good work.

Lessons Learnt

- It is important to understand
    - Why you are doing, what you are doing?
    - Is there is a better way to do things?
- Opportunities are all around us, we need to be able to spot them.
- Never refrain from expressing your opinion. Except for your suggestion being discarded, nothing else can/will go wrong.
- I am sure many of you rather all of you would have or had relevant suggestions. However, generally, two thoughts prevent us from sharing them
    - People will not accept my suggestion
    - It is not a good suggestion

Trust me, early in my career, I used to think the same way and many a time, someone else used to pitch the exact point. Meetings/discussions are meant to share viewpoints and constructively debate about them. All the organisations and leaders want such people in their team who can challenge the status quo and by design enable the group, team and or department to think differently.

CHAPTER 5

Creative Thinking – Sometimes a change in perspective is all that is required

Metaphors are one of the most powerful ways to learn things, to help develop a perspective about situations in life. While they sound good and inspiring, implementing them is generally challenging. Imagine a world wherein human beings do exactly what they preach, the world will be such a wonderful place to live in.

Growing up, one of the metaphors that has fascinated me is - **"Glass is half empty and full at the same**

time". It means that – it is all about the perspective of the person and how he/she sees it. i.e. optimistically (half-full) or pessimistically (half-empty).

In October 2002, I was having a conversation with a friend who had a decent knowledge of astrology, palmistry and numerology. He had been studying these subjects out of curiosity. The conversation was as follows –

Me – Hi Vivek, how are you?

Vivek – Hey, I am doing well. Nothing much, have been busy with the regular stuff. How are you doing?

Me – I am okay too. Just a bit stressed. I am just one month away from my CA final exams and there is so much to do. Honestly speaking, I sometimes feel lost. You cleared your CA in May 2002. Any tips that you would like to share.

Vivek (with a big smile on his face) – CA is such an exam, that I don't feel trips and tricks work. Every attempt is different from the previous one. I even analysed trends but when I went to give the exams, everything changed. In my opinion and with my experience, becoming a CA needs two things – diligence and some luck.

Me – I can and am already to pour in a lot of hard work. I will continue to do so. But I feel that luck is generally not in my control. Let's see what happens.

Vivek – I have some time today. Why don't you give me your date and time of birth? Let me see what numerology has in store for you?

Me – Sounds interesting! But what if there is something that is not in my favour? The only thing I am worried about is that if there is anything negative then what would I do about it.

Vivek – Share the details and let me check. I will come back to you.

I shared my details with him and he promised to come back with his observations by evening. I have noticed (especially amongst Indian students) that during school days and at the time of professional exams, we carry so much burden to perform well which builds unnecessary pressure. And I was no different. I reached home and after lunch, I went back to studies. But my mind was more focussed on what Vivek would have to share. If Vivek shares something positive, it will definitely boost my confidence to put in more efforts.

I kept waiting for his call. There were butterflies in my stomach and curiosity was at its peak.

Back in those days, there were no smartphones and tablets. That was the era wherein landline phones were the only mode of communication. Every time the phone rang, I rushed to pick it, assuming it would be Vivek. He finally called at 6:00 PM. My heartbeat, kind of, raced as he said "Hi".

Me – So what did you infer about me through numerology?

Without wasting any time, I jumped straight to my question.

Vivek – You will surely become a CA.

Me – That surely helps. I have been ingraining a lot of efforts. But what were you able to find out about my CA exams scheduled in November 2002?

Vivek - I studied that as well and there is a slight concern.

Me – Good to hear (sarcastically). And the concern is about?

Vivek – As per numerology, number 4 is not the luckiest number for you. So, if by any chance, your roll number adds up to 4, then there could be a likelihood that you may not become a CA in this attempt. Therefore, you might have to make another attempt at it. However, this is just my observation and I am not 100% sure about it.

Me – Why are you not sure about it?

Vivek – These things are only directional and may or may not be 100% true. I would recommend you to put in your best foot forward and trust in your capabilities.

Me – Thank You Vivek for your efforts. Instead of attaining clarity, I feel more confused now.

We hung up the phone. Whatever Vivek said, got registered in my mind. I was expecting to receive the CA roll number in a week's time. Finally, one afternoon, I got received it through the post. I rushed to open it and totalled the digits. To my surprise and shock, the total of my roll number was 4. I cannot be so unlucky was what I said to myself. I got really upset.

For the next two days, I did not feel like doing anything. I was only 4 weeks away from my exams. I was just not able to concentrate and number 4 had overpowered me in every sense. Thoughts like I should skip my exam this year and attempt my exams next year started coming in.

Mom, just to have a regular chat, came up to check on me if I was studying and feeling okay with my preparations. I did not know if she would feel upset upon learning about my conversation with Vivek. But I just could not keep struggling with my thoughts alone. I needed help. So, I ended up sharing the entire conversation with her. Mom related this entire situation to the glass metaphor to make me understand that there was a 50% chance of what Vivek has predicted was true but the remaining 50% was still in my favour. For either of them to become true, there was only one pre-requisite that I would have to give my exams and for that, I should spend my time studying and not thinking. Her words propped me in gaining the required clarity that my focus should be on the 50% that could be in my favour. I started putting in more efforts and ended up appearing in both the groups; 50% likely and 50% unlikely. In January 2003, I became a CA even though the result was announced on 13th January (again a total of 4) 2003. My efforts out ruled the number 4 theory from my mind forever.

Another metaphor that bears a big impact on me is the one about the shoe salesman. ☺ ☺

A company wanted to set up business in an underdeveloped country. The sales and marketing head identified two salesmen from his team who would be sent to study the market for 2-3 months. Both the salesman returned after 2 months of survey and met the head.

Marketing head asked them to share their findings with the larger team.

Salesman 1 – There is no demand for shoes in this particular country. I covered the length and breadth of the country and everyone seems to be comfortable without shoes. We should focus on some other country and not waste any more time, effort and money here.

Marketing head – Oh, that is not good news. We were banking on this country to boost our exports.

He called the second salesman to know his observation.

Salesman 2 – Sir, my finding is very different and I think there is a huge potential for selling shoes in this country.

Marketing Head – Both of you are sharing a very different perspective of things in the same country. Am I missing something, he asked Salesman 2

Salesman 2 – Let me put it this way sir. There is huge potential to sell shoes in this country and the reason is that currently, no one wears shoes. I carried with me a few pair of shoes and when I offered people to try them out, they felt happy wearing them. Thus, I say that there is a lot of probability to sell shoes.

Marketing Head – That is indeed a brilliant perspective that you have brought into the conversation. I appoint you as the Head of Sales and Marketing for this new country.

Back from the world of metaphors to reality. During my CA days, getting Articleship with a good firm was definitely not easy and I had been waiting for quite some time for the openings to be advertised so I could apply. However, after talking to seniors, I realised that most vacancies for Articleship were not even advertised. Learning from the above, I did some basic maths. I found out approximately the number of:

- Chartered Accountancy firms in the Delhi NCR region
- Number of article assistants that a practicing-chartered accountant can employ under him
- Areas in Delhi NCR with the maximum number of Chartered Accountancy firm

The above analysis was an eye-opener as I realised there were ample opportunities. The only thing I had to do was to find a way to reach out to the firm for my candidature. I printed out several copies of my resume and personally went to hand it over to the HR department or the front office of as many CA firms as I could. Nothing is easy in this world. But who said that just by leaving my resume with multiple firms I would find an Articleship? As NOT expected, I did not get a single call. I understood that for us, our resume is worthwhile but for a chartered accountancy firm, they get flooded with resumes. So next, I decided to follow-up by a phone call with at least 10-15 firms that I had shortlisted for my Articleship.

My strategy paid off and after 2 weeks of rigorous follow-ups, I received calls from 4-5 firms. I went for a personal round of interview and ended up getting selected in 2 of my shortlisted firms. I was delighted and picked one of them to start my Articleship with.

Bottlenecks and problems are a part and parcel of life. They come uninvited almost every time. However, after we learn and practice the art of looking at things from a different lens, we would be able to find hidden opportunities. While working through this process, sometimes you may need help. Believe me – asking for help is not a sign of weakness or incompetence in any manner. I wish we were all competent to solve/do everything on our own. However, the reality is different. If there is a better way of doing things/better advice/more capable people to help you to achieve your goals then ask for it to get things done.

There is a very famous quote – **"We don't see things the way they are, we see things the way we are."** To draw an analogy - people who love photography would understand this better. The ultimate objective is to capture the perfect picture, which lens would do the job for them would need two things –

- An awareness that different lenses exist
- An open mind to be able to try different lenses

Not only personally but professionally also there were several instances in my career when just by changing the perspective, my team and I could deliver and achieve more.

One of the companies that I worked for, once decided to organise their first-ever Innovation & Creativity competition. The idea was to instil the spirit and culture of innovation within the organisation. To do this, there could have been nothing better than encouraging employees to participate in fun games activities and compete in their individual and team capacity. My team (35-40 team members) nominated to participate in full strength with the intent to win the competition. All of them seemed excited.

Amongst the high-energy participants in the room, I observed 2 interns from my team leading from the front. They not only had original and interesting ideas but were also helping other people to make their ideas better. We spent 4-5 hours discussing things. The next day, I called a follow-up meeting. Both the interns raised their hand and said that based on the discussion yesterday and other ideas that we had in mind they had done the following –

- Prepared a list of activities/tasks
- Prepared an overall project plan – days, date, time, etc.

The next task was to identify participants for different games/activities. As a general practice, we would nominate people based on our understanding of them.

However, the interns had a different suggestion. Their idea was to identify people based on their area of interest. One by one people volunteered for their favourite tasks and I could feel a different kind of energy in the room. After all the discussion was over, I asked everyone who should be leading the overall initiative for our team. As expected, the answer was that I should lead it being the "Head of the department".

At the end of the room, I saw two people raising their hands to share their perspectives. Their suggestion was that the initiative should be led by the person who had the maximum understanding of the tasks and had participated in the maximum number of events. It was indeed a brilliant idea. The intent was clearly on winning and we collectively appointed both interns as the leaders of our team. Even I had to follow their instructions and, in all honesty, I was very happy to do that. We had a lot of ups and downs during the competition. We did lose some tasks/activities but in all the major ones, we were in the top 3. Finally, the results were announced and our team had a podium finish. We were number 1. Our interns deserved the maximum applause.

Members from other teams came and said the following –

- We loved the winning spirit of your team.

- We loved your team's open perspective to let people with energy and ideas lead rather than deciding the leader stereotypically based on their designation.

There were smiles all around and I promised to arrange a big treat for the team, especially for our dear interns.

Lessons Learnt

- A negative perception is generally easily available. However, developing a long-term perspective requires experience and maturity.
- Changing the perspective from negative to positive increases the acceptability to solve the situation or take advantage of it.
- Changing the perspective from negative to positive makes the situation look more controllable.
- Bringing in a positive perspective to a difficult situation would require us to disassociate ourselves from the situation.

CHAPTER 6

The Entrepreneurial mindset

Taking the first step in life (personal and professional) is generally the most difficult one. On the professional front, venturing out for my first job seemed like a nightmare for me. During the entire process, I tried to ensure that I kept my guard up all the time and use my time judiciously to learn things relevant to the kind of job I was looking for. After 7 failed attempts, I got my first job offer. On the job learning, having an open mind, etc. continued to be my on-going process for self-improvement.

Right from my first job, working alongside my seniors, I used the following approach –

- To start with, I got a brief understanding of the assignment. In some instances, I was explained the approach for doing the task. Taking ownership of things is more important rather than just doing it as a task that has been assigned to you.
- Next, I combined the briefing with self-research and ensured that the task was completed. Whenever I used to do an assignment, there was a probability that I would face some deadlocks while doing it. In such situations, the recommendation would be to do self-research, either in terms of trying to figure out what needs to be done or identifying the right people who could help.
- I always made it a point to ask my seniors for constructive feedback in terms of how could or what could I have done better. During the process, if they mentioned a few things that I had done well, then it would surely be a cherry on the cake.

In my first 3 jobs, I used the above approach black and white and without any exceptions. It worked well for me. Not only was the feedback from my seniors positive, but I also ensured to work on the constructive feedback that I got. Another key element that helped me, was a skill that I had learnt from my mother, which was to keep my eyes and ears open all the time and observe people and their actions. Trust me, most successful professionals that you would see around have a strong ability to observe.

During my career span of 17+ years, a majority of people I met, believed in doing the task because either a senior had asked them to do it or it was being done previously or it was a part of their job description. The result was that if someone asked detailed questions about the purpose of the task or the task itself, people feel such questions to be out of the syllabus.

In my first job, I was once given the task of preparing the monthly profit and loss and balance sheets using a pre-determined format. The task looked simple to me and I managed to complete it within the stipulated time. As per the initial guidelines, I was required to only populate the numbers in a pre-defined template with numbers. However, since standalone numbers did not communicate a definite meaning to me, I decided to further spend some time to review the numbers and understand trends. While doing this, I was able to spot anomalies in some cases, while for the others, I was able to establish and understand the correlation/ reason for the variation. This made me more comfortable and confident about the assignment.

I emailed the final output to my superior and included additional observations as well. My superior reviewed the tasks and was delighted to see the extra effort that I had brewed in. While reviewing the financial statements, he asked me questions about numbers and trends. My groundwork helped me answer a majority of the questions. I was thrilled with my achievement.

The confidence that I was able to develop, lead me to fetch another exciting opportunity. As part of my next assignment, I was asked to meet a banker. The company that I was working for had applied for loans. For the banker to approve/reject the application, he wanted to develop a better understanding of the financial health of our company – past, present and future (projections). So, he handed over to me a detailed format that was to be populated within a week's timeline. As a chartered accountant, I believe we love to play with numbers.

I immediately sunk my teeth in the format. Within 3 days, I managed to complete it. With 2 days still in hand before my next meeting with the banker, I started analysing numbers, trends and all other analysis that was possible. I documented all of my findings. On the day of the meeting, after I handed over the details to the banker, he explained that one of his team members would analyse the financials and call for further queries. I informed the banker that I had already analysed things in detail and if the team member had a couple of hours, then we could sit together to review. That would not only save their time but also expedite the process. The banker was surprised to hear this. He asked his team members to sit with me for review.

I called to inform my office. The review process which initially had to take a week, got completed on the same day and our company application was ready to be sent to the bank's head office. In a nutshell, I was able to help the company by expediting the process and also build a rapport with the banker. A Win-Win situation for all of us and I felt content about the entire process as it helped me grow as an individual.

To all Millennials wanting and waiting to fast-track their career, my suggestion is –

- What is the task/activity given to you and what is the reason for doing it?
- Who are the users of the task that you are doing? Depending on whether it is an internal/external stakeholder or a client, the perspective could completely change.
- What is the best way to do the task? Even if you know how to do it, it is still advisable to check if there is a better way to do it. This enhances the learning process.
- If it is a task that was being done by someone else in the past, spend some time while going through the working notes, files.
- Prepare your notes on the understanding that you have obtained. There will be gaps and as a result, you may have a lot of questions. Start by a self-research, this not only will you get more

clarity but you will also be able to find some answers.

My leaders were able to spot leadership potential and entrepreneurial ability in me. Every such situation that I took over and was able to execute, prepared me for bigger, broader and deeper roles. Job after job and profile after profile, I did not deviate from this life skill that I had learnt and implemented. As a result, I got opportunities to work on value-added tasks, niche profiles, expand my network of stakeholders and my team became bigger with every role.

As I started to move **"Up The Ladder"**, I continued to polish my entrepreneurial mind-set. Reporting on Key Performance Indicators (KPIs) was an essential part of my role. At the start of every year, I used to formulate my annual goals with my manager. We have all been taught that goals should be framed using the "SMART" framework. However, for my personal growth, I improvised and added two additional elements for myself – I expanded **"SMART"** to be **"SMAARTE".** The additional A and E for me were – Ambitious and Entrepreneurial. I took on this personal challenge and, in the process, I have been fine-tuning to a better version of myself both personally and professionally.

Take a moment and think about it. To be an entrepreneur, it is not always essential to have your own enterprise. We just need an entrepreneurial mindset.

Role after role, I held on to the entrepreneurial mindset which in turn enabled me to achieve personal and professional growth. Instead of

- Reporting key performance indicators, I started working to improve them
- Being a finisher of tasks, I started working on the process of ideation
- Accepting tasks, I started making suggestions/recommendations to stakeholders
- Rather than doing all tasks myself, I delegated more to actively involve team members in the review process
- Obtaining targets and achieving them, I started recommending targets
- Instead of or despite the business deciding when to work and on what areas to work, I proactively started working on business development
- Selling services, I started selling solutions based on the need of the stakeholders
- Working on a "What will succeed approach", I shifted to "What can go wrong approach" to make the concept more fool proof

Organisations generally are supportive of this mindset and have been diligently working to empower employees to make decisions. We just need to start feeling that we are an entrepreneur.

Even while you are in an employee-employer relationship, you can still work as an entrepreneur and manage different aspects of the business.

- Entrepreneurship, in my opinion, is a mind-set.
- Entrepreneurship needs to be inculcated from within you. Start feeling like an entrepreneur even when you are an employee and actively contribute to the growth of the business.
- 'Entrepreneurs are not made in a day'. They learn to crawl, walk, run and finally fly to ultimately reach their destination. I have interacted with many successful professionals from different careers and all of them have this characteristic in common – They take their job as if they are running their own venture.

Leaders of organisations are entrepreneurs. Star-performers in a team are generally people with an entrepreneurial mindset and a high-performing team is a combination of multiple entrepreneurial employees who walk the extra mile.

Lessons Learnt

- It is important to keep your mind open, curiosity active and energy levels high.
- Completing the task is important but how it is done is even more important.
- Experience comes through active experimentation. The number of years may define the duration of experience but not the depth of it.
- To be an entrepreneur, you don't have to wait to be called one. Start feeling it and you will see the difference.
- An entrepreneur takes charge of things and situations, without being asked to so.
- Focus on the bigger picture.
- Craft situations and lead people to find solutions. Enable people to become problem-solvers rather than solving problems on their behalf.
- Entrepreneurs are change-agents both within and outside the organisation.

CHAPTER 7

Your Vision - Your Guiding Light

was fortunate to have become a CA at the age of 22.5 years with an All India Rank of 34. Friends and family were all happy and they congratulated me. I was on cloud nine and felt like I was all set for brighter horizons. I started dreaming about having a great career start. When we think we have a plan for life, life becomes smarter and throws a new challenge at us. I wanted to make it big in the corporate world and dreamt of becoming a CEO (Chief Executive Officer) in the future.

If we study well in school, it opens our door to a good college. Similarly, when we study in college, we feel that it opens a gateway to a good job. So, I harboured the notion that getting a good job would come to me by default.

My batch mates who unfortunately could not pass the exam had to re-study and re-appear for the exams. I felt bad for them. But I was sure that with their hard work, they will make it through. Even with a rank up my sleeve, to my surprise, finding a job was not that easy. Probably either my resume was not being screened properly or I was not posting it on the right portal; I was uncertain of the actual reason. I was getting a little impatient to start my career.

Finally, as part of the campus placement process, I started getting calls from companies. I was happy and at the same time, a bit nervous too. I prepared for the interviews (no matter how well-prepared we are before an exam we still keep revising the syllabus and still have the fear of having missed out on any chapter). In total, 7 companies interviewed me. I was confident in my capabilities. But a whip of reality-check awakened me from my reverie when I could not make it to any one of them. I was shocked and devasted. While I prepared for the interview, I did not prepare for the failure. I did not know what was lacking. Tragically, life, for me, came to a standstill. I had no clue what to do next. Fortunately or unfortunately, I was the 1st Chartered Accountant in my entire family and I wanted to prove, not to anyone but myself. I promised myself that no matter what, I would not give up, as giving up did not exist in our family's morals/values.

I aggressively started to apply for more jobs through various job portals, consultants, etc. But I was not getting calls and everything seemed stuck. Guess, as a 22-year-old, who did not know much about corporate, expected that on the very next day HR should call me and confirm that my resume was shortlisted. If they did not call, it meant that my resume was not accepted. This carried on for another few days. My morale seemed to be nosediving but my mom's support kept me going.

On a late Thursday afternoon, I got a call for an interview from a lady called Vandana. While I saw a wick of hope, I was very scared due to my series of failures. As I could not let this opportunity leak out, I spent the entire night preparing for the interview. The next day, I reached the office well before time and waited for my turn to meet the CFO Mr. Jain (the interviewer). While I was waiting, I looked around the office and the employees who passed by. During that waiting period, a thought that surfaced in my mind was "Will I get the opportunity to work with this organisation and some of the people I saw?" As the drone of thought circled around my head, I heard the HR calling my name. I, in an instant, picked my bag, remembered God and entered the meeting room. Mr. Jain stood up, shook hands and greeted me with a smile. He made me feel comfortable by asking me some general questions like how was I doing, etc. and then followed the real questions. As the interview progressed, my nervousness got the better of me. Some questions that I answered were incorrect and, in a few others, I literally froze. Finally, the interview ended and I was told that they will get back to me with the results. I went back home puzzled, not knowing what the results would be.

Every time the phone rang, I would run to pick it up with the hope that it would be a call from the HR. Some interview results are declared then and there. But when you are told that HR will get back to you, it has 2 meanings – either you are selected or they will interview other candidates and then share the results. So, here I had to wait for the call.

A week later, I finally got a call from the HR. I crossed my fingers before the result was shared with me. They declared that I was selected. I just could not hold the excitement to share the news with my family. As soon as the call ended, I sprinted to my family members and told them about my selection. After those episodic failures, it was like a drowning man catching at a straw. They were all so happy for me as they always knew I will make it. I collected my offer letter and this marked the start of my professional career. There was no looking back thereafter.

Time flew and I had completed 8 successful years in the corporate world. Work became worship for me. In between, some good opportunities came my way and I availed them. I used to dream, eat, sleep, breathe and love work. To-do list, projects, deliverables, stakeholders, targets, initiatives, etc. – My life had become a corporate dictionary.

One day (when I was working with the shared service centre of an MNC bank), my boss Mr. Gupta called me and asked for a coffee break. Those of you who have some financial service experience would know how hectic and busy the month-end, quarter-end or year-end reporting cycles are. It was a quarter-end cycle for us and that was my 1st coffee break in 6 hours. I went down to the cafeteria, which was also our assembly point. As we were guzzling our coffee, Mr. Gupta asked me "How are things going?" My usual reply being – All is Well. After chit-chatting about a few other things, Mr. Gupta finally shared the breaking news. He told me about an international project; a project if I got selected for, I would have to stay in Canada for about 18 months. The cherry on the cake was – if I delivered the project successfully, I might get a chance (if I wanted) to stay back in Canada.

I was not good at painting or else, I would have painted all the imaginations that were dancing in my mind at that very moment. I was cruising through the images of frolic. It was always my dream to go and settle abroad.

However, this was not the 1st time when I was eyeball-to-eyeball with my dream. My boss asked me to take the time, think about it and come back to him. The timing was perfect as, by that time, our coffee mugs had no more coffee left. I shook hands with him and took the stairs to my desk. I was glad that I had finished most of my work for the day and could not wait to go home. Despite living in the world of technology, I resisted the temptation to send a message to mom and sister.

A hurricane of emotions was flaring up in my mind, so instead of taking the cab for home, I decided to go down for a solo walk. To me, talking always helped. I always wanted to settle abroad but this time, for some strange reason the opportunity did not seem very lucrative to me. I have always been a restless soul trying to do many things, but somehow, I was thoroughly confused within.

After returning from the walk, I finally packed my bag and got inside the company cab to go back home. Friends who know me well also know that I rarely sit quietly in the cab. However, that was the day when I sat hushed. Old melodies that were playing on a radio channel felt soothing and I slept. After an hour's drive, I reached home. It was about 10:15 PM. Mom served me the dinner and I shared about the Canada project with her. Mom congratulated me and said, "Your expressions do not reconcile with your feelings, so let us talk in the morning." She was so right about how I was feeling.

I don't remember even a single episode in my career that happened without discussing or consulting with her. We both had our opinions and we agreed to disagree most of the time. After a good, healthy discussion with her, I used to take my own sweet time to process, maybe to gather more data and if required talk more about it either with her or sometimes through self-talk. Over time, I have understood that when we are in a situation we feel strongly about, it becomes difficult to disassociate with it to be able to evaluate the pros and cons. I was no different and thus talking helped me go ahead with the plan. Discussions always give a perspective and many times it unveils a dimension that we may have not thought about.

The next morning being a Saturday and the weekly off from work, Mom, sister and I sat down for a discussion. I shared the details about the opportunity that I had got. Mom said she was waiting to hear about the dilemma that had dropped anchor in my mind. I immediately said that I did not want to opt for the opportunity. Both mom and sister looked bewildered, but I kept talking. I said that while the opportunity was good, it did not add up well to what my long-term goals were. The funny thing was that I hated mathematics, but that day, I was talking about addition and that too about things in life. I said that I needed to upskill myself to fulfil my dream. Mom knew there was more to come and when I get full attention from both the ladies, I never stop talking. I told them that I wanted to get back to my studies. I felt the need to broaden my horizon and equip myself with more accreditations. Trust me, it was not at all an easy decision to make.

Each one of you might have or would be facing such crossroad situations. Here, my recommendation would be to take your time, evaluate the pros and cons and remember your 'personal vision statement'. Your decisions need to be aligned to your personal vision statement and if you are confident about it then back yourself up.

I went to my boss on the following Monday and declined the offer. He asked me to order a large cup of coffee that day as the conversation was going to be a long one. As we sat down to discuss, I explained to him about my aspirations and the overall plan. I expected him to get upset but on the contrary, he boosted my confidence and told me that I was making the right decision.

It always helps to take your seniors, mentors and family members into confidence. While on one hand, you get their perspective on things, on the other hand, they give you all the support possible.

I started looking for another job and also began my research about courses that would equip me with the knowledge that I needed to accelerate in the future. In the next few months, I got myself enrolled in the courses – an executive MBA from IIFT and CIMA (UK). I switched to an organisation that was close to my place so that I could save time on my commute and use that time to study instead.

Stephen Covey in his book "7 Habits of Highly Effective People" has emphasized on this important element. Everyone should work to "Sharpen their Saw". Successful companies and professionals both have one thing in common; they continuously assess/re-assess their vision statement and make changes if required. They not only try to make the right choices but also ensure effective implementation.

My new learning created a new set of opportunities. The tools and techniques that I had learnt seemed so very relevant in my new role in the organisation. I entered the league of strategy-formulators in my organisation – a role that I was aspiring to take and I was now right into it – Strategic management. Personally, for me, this was a big leap forward.

Still, a mild smile appears when I see and read about Canada. I will surely go there one day (even if it is on a vacation). However, that smile turns into an ear-to-ear smug when I think about the opportunities that opened up for me with that one Big and Bold decision of my life.

My advice to all the professionals (especially the Millennials) is that you should '***continue to re-invent yourself***'.

Lessons Learnt

- Practice the art of self-talk, so is talking to your family and mentors. Self-awareness about the environment backed up by strong research are essential ingredients to make a good decision.
- Write down, re-visit and amend your personal vision statement. You may need to change the path or accelerate your journey towards your destination.
- What tastes good might not be healthy. Do not stop yourself from trying what does not initially taste/feel good. It may be the recipe for a better you and also a better life.
- Sometimes your temptations might resist you. Many times, you have to resist temptation.
- Think and Act Long-Term.

CHAPTER 8

The Game Changer – Be Consistently Progressive

After finishing lap 2, my sister (Geetanjali) was in 7th place amongst 15 runners who were competing for a podium finish in a 2000 metre race. She started accelerating in lap 3. I had closely watched her during her practice sessions and I knew that her major acceleration would come in the final 2 laps. Now at the end of lap 4, she was at number 4. The runners ahead of her were tiring out due to short booster sprints multiple times in every lap. As soon as lap 5 (final lap) started, Geetanjali started accelerating and made all her house members sit on the edge of their chairs. She was very much in the hunt for a medal.

Till this time, honestly, even I was getting irritated and wanted her to accelerate earlier. She was now at 3 and had started inching closer to the runner at the number 2 position. Even I started running with her on the inner track and kept shouting at the top of my voice "Buck up Geetanjali, you can win the race." She surely had an adrenalin rush and all her housemates started cheering for her in chorus. Not only did she inject more power but her long legs started taking longer and faster strides. It was getting close with 100-150 metres remaining. Out of nowhere, she pressed on the accelerator and there she was, now at 1st position and in the pursuit of a gold medal. Geetanjali has always been cool as a cucumber and puts her strategy to perfect execution. We were all very happy.

That same evening, Mom, Geetanjali and I were sitting in the balcony. My sister had won a major track and field event a few hours ago and I had lost one on the same day. Geetanjali was always a rhythmic and long-distance runner as compared to me who was an impulsive sprinter. Mom asked me "Do you know why you did not win?" I said, "Because others were faster than me." I also said that I lost due to the fact that right before the race, I had practiced a lot. It tired me and downgraded my energy level for the ultimate race. Mom looked at me and said that those could also be the reasons, but the real reason was something different. She said that I was Not Consistent with my practice. On the face, I did not agree with what mom said, but deep down inside me, I knew that mom was bang on.

We all learn most of our life lessons and skills while we are in school. Our parents at home and teachers in the school are the ones who give us most of our learning. In class 12th, despite my mom warning me of my inconsistency in studies, I did not take it seriously. I was shattered after my class 12th result. The result was twofold – Not only I got marks that were below my expectation but my dream of getting into Shri Ram College of Commerce (SRCC) also got shattered. In fact, I could not get into any of my top 5 dream colleges in Delhi University. All I wanted at that time was a time machine and if I could go back in time, I would do one thing differently. I would be consistent and this was what I said to myself after ruminating over my 12th score.

Learning a foreign language was something that really wanted to do and I signed up for the classes. However, I did not revise at home and rather catapulted the excuse that I was very busy at work. The result was that I gave up on the classes despite the fact that the fee I had paid was non-refundable. Till today, I carry the grudge that if only I had been consistent, I would have been an expert in French language and my market value as a professional would have definitely been a few notches higher.

> **"The Short and Long Route to Success in Life is based on only 1 principle – Consistency." – Akhil Iyer**

We are the generation of Social Media - a generation of likes, emojis, followers and status stories. Our world seems highly virtual but yet deeply aspirational. Today, being on every social media platform is a must.

Social media has given us the power to build the brand called "ME" which can be truly global. I personally chose to build my brand on 'LinkedIn'. While I created my account on the platform a couple of years back but I never used it.

It was in November 2019, I was using my new smartphone, trying to download different 'Apps' from Google Play Store when I saw LinkedIn. I started using it. For the next 2-3 days, I read a lot on LinkedIn – Articles, Posts and short stories. A few of my friends messaged me "Welcome Back". While reading people's stories, I said to myself 4 things –

- I also have similar stories
- I also want to write and share with the world
- It does not look difficult
- It looks interesting as we could get connected to people across the globe and it would be a tremendous opportunity to learn

The next day, I decided to write something. As it is said *taking the first step is the most difficult one*, I felt as if I had taken out an old typewriter from the closet, removed dust from it and was ready to start typing. I started to write and after a few iterations, I posted my first post. I felt good! ☺

As soon as I clicked on the post button, I got a message on the screen saying "posted successfully". I kept looking at the screen and kept refreshing it. Slowly I saw that a few people had viewed my post. However, none of them clicked on the like button. I started thinking in my mind that maybe people did not like what I had written. After the first hour, I got 2 reactions. That was enough for me to be happy about, so I started thinking about what to write next.

On the same day a friend, Amit called me and said he had read my post. Amit was candid enough to say that he did not like the post. He went on to ask me

- How many views did the post get – I said 74
- How many reactions did the post get – I said 7

His next few words demotivated me and I got really upset. I saw my post several times after the conversation but there was hardly any change in the statistics. The next morning, I felt like writing again. I decided to write again and this time if my friend would ask me about how well my post did, I had thought of an answer as well – ***"I write to express and not to impress."***

Amit did not call. As compared to last time, my post did better. I started spending more time on the platform – Reading posts, sharing my thoughts and even writing. Selecting a topic initially was difficult but slowly I had a list of topics to write about. I spent 3-4 hours daily on the platform and started posting content twice every week.

I started understanding the finer details of hashtag, followers, views, reactions, trending posts, comments, re-shares and much more.

I have now been writing for more than 10 months. The journey has been full of learning and rewarding at the same time. While I continue to build and strengthen my brand, I have made a point to celebrate a few milestones as well. Building your "Brand" is very important for every professional irrespective of the degrees and the number of years of experience that you have in your armoury.

As they say, 'Rome was not built in a day', nothing (Brand, company, career, etc.) gets built in a single day. It needs several hours of consistent effort for days and maybe months. There will always be ups and downs in whatever we do. However, it is super critical to stay put and keep moving forward.

Be it my 17+ years of corporate journey or the second innings of my career (which I have just begun), my priority has always been to **"Be Consistent"**. Having worked with several young professionals, I always encourage them to focus on being consistent. The outcome is a direct result of efforts. If the efforts are not consistent then the output (most likely) will be below expectations.

Over the last 10 months, I have raised my personal bar of being consistent and trust me, it is yielding results as well. If it can work for me, it can work for anyone and in anything that we wish to do. Even the world takes note of your consistency and provides you with consistent opportunities as well.

Think about your favourite brands. One of the key elements that differentiate them from others is Consistency in whatever they do. Your brand reaches:

- Places and People before you think you can reach there.
- Places and People where you may never even think of going.
- Places and People who you might not be even aware of.

I interact with many people on a daily basis, mostly first-time conversations. I get to hear from people that they have been reading my posts, stories and articles on LinkedIn. The biggest victory for me is when people tell me that because of my consistency in posting content, they are consistent in reading it. Some of them even knew that my content generally comes out every Monday and Thursday. Consistency can and will always be the game-changer, no matter what you do.

Let us look at the results of being consistent:

- 10k+ followers (from under 500 to 10k in only 10 months)
- 1.5 million views
- 40% Reactions (% of views)
- 60/100 Posts have trended under different hashtags (%)

Based on the successful people whom I have observed and also those who I have mentored, one quality that stands out is their relentless focus to **"Be Consistent"**. It helps in building and sustaining your brand in a more effective manner. A strong brand helps you in getting more opportunities than what you can think of.

Recently when I gave up on my corporate journey, I was not worried about the next innings of my life. I know that my mantra for success would be driven through my life skill of being consistent with my efforts in whatever I plan to do. The good news is that in less than 3 months, I am already in discussion with people to explore and finalise prospective opportunities.

Lessons Learnt

- Nothing comes easy in life.
- Be consistent in whatever you do and you will surely grow. Inconsistency, on the other hand, pulls you down.
- Despite the detractors in your life, keep moving ahead.
- Break your larger goals into smaller actionable ones. Hold yourself accountable or appoint someone to hold you accountable. In my case, my sister holds me accountable to take consistent action.
- Your goals can be ambitious. But remember that ONLY consistent efforts will make them realistic.
- Celebrate smaller milestones.

CHAPTER 9

Imagine to Re-Imagine – If you can visualise it, you can achieve it

When I was a kid, I had this habit of talking to myself. To me, self-talk was a powerful way to express things that were there in my mind. I used to feel relieved and it also helped me in finding answers to my questions or at the least have better clarity about what was manifesting in my mind.

I still remember Swami Vivekananda's quote that I came across during my childhood days, "Talk to yourself at least once in a day, otherwise, you may miss meeting with an excellent person in this world."

Every commerce student who dreams of becoming a chartered accountant would resonate with me when I say that despite being one of the most challenging courses, CA is also the most rewarding course for finance professionals in India. I started my journey through the CA foundation route in 1998. I had to clear 4 papers to go to the next level. My first three exams went well. The last paper was economics and because I loved the subject, I thought it would be a cakewalk for me. However, in the evening, I suddenly started to panic. I still don't know the reason. It could be because of exertion as I had been putting in long study hours for a few months or it could also be due to the pressure of the exam itself.

Eventually, I decided to give up on the economics exam. I told mom about my situation and went off to sleep. Mom would never let me give up without trying. She sat beside me and kept reading the notes to me. I woke up after a few hours and realised that I only had 3-4 hours to complete the revision. She used the **"Imagine to Re-Imagine"** technique and made me believe that I could still do it. For all practical reasons, I learnt that even **"God helps those who help themselves".**

I was now pumped up to complete the revision and finish my exam. Two months later, the results were declared and I had cleared level 1 of CA.

I have noticed with a lot of people around that as we grow in age, we tend to lose sight of some of our good habits which used to work very well for us. As soon as I started working, I got so busy that I started losing sight of my real aspirations. My advice to all the Millennials would be to never lose sight of your aspirations as it will keep you motivated.

One of my friends (including me) had been thinking about writing a book for almost 2-3 years. Initially, the idea was to write a book on technical topics based on our experience of teaching professional courses and I had also started writing it. After scribbling a few pages, we dropped the idea. Either we were not convinced about what, how we wanted to write or rather we had become too lazy to continue writing. In our case, the power of excuse was stronger than our conviction to write. In fact, we were more than convinced that writing was not our cup of tea. A small obstacle and we hurl our dream out of the window. If it is so easy to let go of your dream, then it is actually not a dream in the first place.

As **Dr. A P J Abdul Kalam** sir has rightly said – **"Dreams are not those that come to you while you are sleeping. Dreams are those that do not let you sleep."**

Thereafter, life continued as usual. One day, I was conducting an introductory session for new joiners (mostly freshers) in my team. I started with an icebreaker activity to make them feel comfortable and be able to build a rapport with them. That session also gave them an opportunity to ask any questions that were there in their mind. In case I did not have answers to certain questions, I promised to circle back to them. It started as a regular conversation with everyone sharing a few things about themselves. This was followed by some overview of the process. Before the end of the session, now that everyone felt more comfortable, a few participants who were curious to know more about me asked me about:

- My professional journey so far
- 3-4 skills that I thought would help them grow in the company and in their career overall

I could have spent the entire day talking about both these things. My day at work was a bit light. However, answering their questions seemed more important, so I decided to spend a couple of extra minutes. With limited time in hand, I spoke less about my professional journey and more about the skills that could help the new joiners settle well in their roles.

After the discussion concluded, they recommended me to write a book to share the skills with more and more professionals especially the Millennials. I smiled and finally, the session concluded. The dream of writing a book (this time non-technical) got reignited. That day during lunch, my managers enquired about the session.

I shared that it went well and the participants recommended me to write a book. ☺

On my way back home, I again kept thinking about the idea of writing a book. I know you must be thinking that maybe I was getting too carried away with the outcome of the meeting in terms of the importance of life skills not only for the participants but also for many more Millennials in their pursuit of a great career. Thoughts about my previous attempt to write a book also started to cross my mind. I was still an hour away from reaching home. Generally, I would spend most of my time chit-chatting with fellow cab mates. However, that day, I rather decided to re-instate my technique of **"Imagine to Re-Imagine"**.

I closed my eyes and started thinking of the time when I would complete my book and it would be ready for the launch. I would hold my first book in my hand. It would be a book with a beautifully designed cover, good layout and impressive printing. I could see that my friends, family and colleagues would also be present at the launch ceremony. Powerful visuals started projecting in front of my eyes as I envisaged un-wrapping my book amidst a nonstop photoshoot with applauses all around. I would personally sign all copies of the book and hand them over to the readers. It will surely be a mega-launch on all social media platforms. Hoping that readers would like the book, my book could be a #No1 Bestseller as well. I felt amazed and my dream seemed like a reality waiting to unfold. By this time, I reached home, I felt positive and happy.

There could have been times when you imagined about starting to work on your dream/aspiration/ambition. However, because of certain bottlenecks, you may have given up the dream. I was a perfect example of this. To all you Millennials, I would strongly urge you to practice this technique of **"Imagine to Re-imagine"** and notice the difference that it will bring. Practice it and make this technique your habit/second nature.

I am generally asked this question - How does this technique work? When to use this technique? So, the answer is, you re-imagine:

- Your future
- Your success
- Your glory
- Your celebration
- Your appreciation
- Your applause
- Your name and fame

In short, for anything that you wish to achieve in life.

You will feel that you have already achieved your dream through the power of visualization. Try doing it now, before reading any further. Did you feel goosebumps, did you feel an electric current passing through your body? If you felt it, let me ask you a simple question - Is it worth making efforts for what you just Re-imagined? If you can visualise it then:

- It is a real dream/ambition/aspiration
- It indicates that you feel strongly about it and you own the dream
- Taking action becomes much easier

This is not an affirmation. This is visualising your dream and seeing it turn into reality. If you can see it and feel it, then you will surely make efforts to achieve it as well.

I have used this several times and it has worked wonders. It enables you to "Nurture" hope and action when you feel down and under. Whenever you feel under pressure, whenever you feel like giving up on something close to your heart, whenever you feel demotivated due to obstacles, close your eyes and use the technique. Visualise how you would feel when you will achieve success. Be descriptive in your imagination. Imagine big, imagine large, imagine the grandeur and imagine all the minute details. The more powerful your imagination is, the more success would mean to you and the more will be your efforts in achieving them.

A few months back, I used this technique again. The outcome was I took a bold decision to give up on my corporate career at a time when I was at my peak. I wanted to be a Coach, Mentor and Storyteller. So far, I was doing it as a hobby, but now I wanted to make my hobby as my job. The decision had its consequences:

- From an Assistant Director to Mr. Nobody
- From leading a team of 150+ professionals to being a one-man army
- From a handsome six-figure salary to surviving on minuscule savings.

But honestly, I feel richer, I have more peace of mind and I am happier than I was before.

My career span across 7 large companies played a significant role in shaping me as a person. However, the entire journey seemed to me like a vicious circle – I got one thing and I desired for one more. I was like a dog (by the way I love dogs) stuck in the loop of wanting to break free. This time, it was "Now" or "Never" for me. I took the plunge. Luckily family and friends responded affirmatively.

When I gave up my job to pursue my passion, I did not think about "Can Do" or "Can't Do", I just told myself, I want to "TRY Doing It", I want to "TRY to Achieve It" and I want to "TRY Making It Happen".

Coincidentally, I am at a stage where the "Eagle" (the most royal bird) is when she ages. Rather than accepting the life she has, she decides to "Re-invent" herself. She breaks her beak and waits for a "New" and "Sharper" beak. She uses the new beak to pluck her

"Old" and "Heavy" feathers and waits for "New Feathers" to live her "New Life" and infinite "Newer Flights". This is a perfect example of the technique of **"Imagine to Re-Imagine".**

When I would leave the world for good, I don't want to leave behind a legacy of wealth. Rather I want to leave behind a legacy of:

- "Chasing" and "Achieving" dreams
- "Inspiring" others to take action
- My stories relating to "Failures" and "My Learnings" from them

Lessons Learnt

- Take a moment and reflect on the habits that you had as a child and later in the mayhem of so many things around you, you lost sight of them.
- Take the next step, write them down and make a promise to use them.
- Imagine success (including a fast-track career) and things become much clearer to you. When you immerse yourself in the feeling of visualising what success would look like when you achieve it, your zeal to make efforts overpowers the power of your excuses and/or bottlenecks around.

- The human brain acknowledges, processes and retains visuals more than text at any given point in time. With deeper involvement, aggressive and diligent action, you can fast-pace your journey towards success

- Whenever you feel you are losing it or going down, spend a few minutes to use the technique of **"Imagine to Re-Imagine"**. My friends and I have used it several times and it works. It helps you stay closer to your aspirations and work your way through all the stumbling blocks as well.

CHAPTER 10

Resist temptations – Always Think, Plan and Execute for the Long Term

We were a family of 4 – my parents, a younger sister and I. My mother used to take coaching classes at home. She was highly loved and hugely respected by all her students. Coaching kids was her hobby. We were happy in our simple and beautiful life.

My father was a simple person. He was not expressive when it came to conveying his feelings. He was the main bread-earner of our family. He liked to socialise but when it came to friends, he had two close friends.

One fine evening in the year 1996, he expressed his desire to venture out and set up his own business. This came as a breaking news for us. Never before had he expressed that he wanted to get into business. In fact, from the lens of past discussions at home, it seemed he was always happy with his job. We all sat down to discuss the feasibility of this decision as a family. His plan was to set up a company trading in steel tubes and pipes. He wanted to leverage his product knowledge and relationships in this area given his vast experience of working with steel tube and pipe manufacturing companies. The proposal looked good and he sounded very convincing while he explained things to us.

When we enquired about his instant decision of switching from service to business, he mentioned that since two of his friends were venturing into business, it was a good opportunity for him as well. His reply triggered further questions in our mind. "In case the business does not go as per plan is there a plan B in place," we asked. Given that he had no alternate plan, we suggested that he should be open to going back to a 9 AM – 5 PM job again. He maintained silence as a response to this suggestion.

As a family, we always encouraged each other in life. However, that was a big decision and we were sceptical if it did not go well then it would close all the doors for us. I was not even matured enough to understand the planning process that dad had followed – I mean did he go through any kind of checklist? That was a thought running through my mind.

Discussions continued for a couple of days at home, however, it seemed that dad had already taken the plunge. As a family, we decided to support him. A major portion of the savings we had was now invested in his business. He worked long hours to establish his business. He had already prepared us mentally that it would take a while for the business to reach a break-even point. He started getting customers for his products. A few months after he started the business, he was also able to crack two big deals. This not only lifted my dad's confidence and but ours as well. To fulfil these orders, he further invested our family's personal savings into business with a promise to re-instate all the savings once he received payment from his buyers. A 90-day grace period was given to the buyers for making the payment. However, they were like fly-by-night companies. As the time to make the payment was nearing, we got to know that the buyers vanished overnight. It looked like the end of the world to us and we were completely shattered.

Every individual and family have a defined risk appetite, keeping in mind their needs. Going any step further is like falling in a trap of temptation. This is exactly what had happened to us. More than us, I felt that my dad got shaken and he went completely silent. As a family, we tried to motivate him and make him understand that he should consider going back to an office job. For him, going back to a regular job meant that he would have to face embarrassment. He wanted some time to come out of it.

In the interim, my mom decided to take charge of the situation. To better our financial health, she started increasing the number of coaching classes that she took. Instead of teaching kids for 2 hours per day, she extended it to 7-8 hours. She has always had natural leadership qualities with a never-give-up attitude. I saw her balancing everything to perfection.

Deep down in my heart and mind, I felt the responsibility to support my parents. In those days doing a part-time job in a fast-food outlet was trending. I felt tempted for the sole reason that whatever I would be able to earn, it would not only enable me to pay for my coaching but also provide some financial support to my family. Here I was - face-to-face with temptation.

Without informing mom, I went to give an interview and test my luck. The interview was a quick process and I also got selected. I was happy with my achievement; I was extremely excited to share this news with mom and see the happiness that would reflect on her face.

I went home and shared the news with her. She congratulated me on my 1st interview success and felt proud of me acting maturely. Thereafter, the first question she asked was "What prompted you to take this step?" Her simple intent was to understand if I felt any kind of financial pressure that forced me to find a job.

One week after joining the job, I realised that I was not able to diligently focus on my studies. Attending classes, finishing school homework and simultaneously working drained my energy. I decided to discuss the situation with my mom. She made me understand that temptation of any kind will definitely look good in the short run. However, we need to focus on the long-term goal. The message was loud and clear to me. I left my fast food job the very next day. Had my dad not fell for his temptation, maybe I would have not learnt an important life skill; a life skill learnt the hard way.

Later in the corporate world, I heard of these two terms – Band-Aid approach and a Wellness program. As the name suggests, the band-aid is a short-term solution to a problem whereas, a wellness program is more fundamental and long-term in nature. When I relate these two terms in my case

- Working at a fast-food joint was the Band-Aid approach.
- Focusing on studies by **resisting the temptation** of any kind was a wellness program.

In my experience, I observed two different types of professionals and temptations -

- Professionals who genuinely want to do a particular thing but don't end up doing it. This is because either they do not have clarity about the task or they feel that it may not help them in achieving their more important, tangible and short-term results such as promotion, bonus and increment. A perfect example of temptation.
- Professionals who are given opportunities to excel but they are so comfortable in their comfort zone that they generally do not engage in any differential and/or agile learning. Being in your comfort zone is also a temptation.

There is no defined temptation for an individual as it varies from individual to individual, depending on their circumstances. I have been no different and some of my temptations later included:

- Foreign travel for an assignment.
- Working with the intent to get promoted, which means higher tangible monetary benefits such as increment and bonus.
- Completing 5 years in an organisation would mean eligibility for Gratuity.

There is no harm in working towards all of this.

My corporate temptations kept me away from pursuing my passion. This time, it was now or never and finally, I decided to take the "Leap of Faith". I had built a corporate legacy and this time, I wanted to build my personal legacy. Eventually, in April 2020, I bid goodbye to the corporate world.

Lesson Learnt

- Short cuts will seem lucrative and may even give you faster results sometimes. However, from a long-term perspective, we surely need to avoid any such temptations.
- Temptations will always surround us and appear to be reassuring. Sustain strong will power and the impact of temptation will fade away.
- Temptations are applicable to individuals, teams and even to a company as a whole.
- If you really don't want to fall into the trap of temptation then inculcate the habit to discuss and listen with an open mind.
- Thinking, planning and executing with long-term in mind is the best counter to temptation.

Excerpts based on interviews conducted with Top Professionals

---

Debotri Dhar (Ph.D., Author, Core Faculty at University of Michigan)

The journey has been very interesting, to say the least! From a small high school, to making it to one of Delhi University's most prestigious colleges, to going to England and earning a Masters with distinction from Oxford University, to coming to the United States, completing a Ph.D., living and working here for the last several years, speaking at Ivy Leagues and authoring many books that are read around the world, it has perhaps been more than she imagined.

Yes, in the beginning, it certainly felt like she was trying to juggle careers in two different fields –

academia and creative writing. But over time, she learned to reconcile them in ways that do not feel as disconnected. For instance, she writes novels, short stories, essays and newspaper columns as a writer; while as an academic, teaches (at the University of Michigan, USA, where she holds a full-time position as core faculty) and publishes scholarly research. Her recent book **"Love is Not a Word"**, which has scholarly essays but a worth-read for the general public.

She has been invited to present her work by universities like Harvard and Yale, has done books for renowned world publishers like Bloomsbury London and New York, has served as an expert in various national and international capacities and has also been written about in newspapers around the world.

Her biggest achievement is that she has been able to craft a life where she genuinely enjoys her work (which for her is more than just a career. It is passion, vocation.) Secondly, the love of her students, readers, creative communities and anyone who looks up to her or is inspired by her.

She believes that one should have a vision in life, a personal value system, work hard towards goals and persist in the face of failure (which come in every person's life).

Top 3 Life skill choices - Life may not give 2 chances – You need to have 2 or more plans instead, Resist temptations and Plan for the Long-Term and Creative Thinking – Sometimes a change in perspective is all that is required. Planning in a way that you have plan B, plan C, etc. is important (even though life may sometimes interrupt with our best-laid plans!). Planning is important for the long-term, and being able to choose work that you are passionate about. This is what genuinely fills you with joy and allows you to be self-actualized.

Message to Millennials - *Have faith in yourself and do not get so absorbed towards the destination of fast-tracking your career that you forget to enjoy the journey.*

Charu Mittal (Director Finance at Korn Ferry)

Her experience spans more than 2 decades with companies such as **PWC, American Express and Korn Ferry**. Since her childhood days, she aspired to be a Chartered Accountant. There was a time, she was the only female Chartered Accountant in Aligarh. Later, she moved to Delhi and joined PWC. Despite her initial failure, she never gave up and became a result-oriented professional.

She continuously expanded her zone of influence by asking the right questions, putting in extra efforts to convert her weakness into strengths and expanding her breadth of learning.

Ideating simple solutions for complex problems, agility to transition into new and diverse roles, ability to think and work as a business partner and delivering to commitments have been the key ingredients for her success.

Top 3 Life skill choices – Celebrate Failure, Challenge the status quo and Connecting the Dots.

Message to Millennials – Organisations are adapting themselves to create a culture that would allow you to learn and fill in leadership positions. However, it is equally essential for Millennials to demonstrate agile leaning to ensure fitment in a fast-paced and unstructured environment. Commitment to goals, seamless delivery, resilience and perseverance would be non-negotiable.

Kshama Dhir (Partner, EY GDS TAS)

Her experience spans more than 2 decades at senior positions with companies including **GE, Colt, Countrywide and EY.**

For the first 3-4 years, despite the unconscious bias against women workers, societal pressure, working long hours and frequent travel, she kept proving herself and marching forward. Slowly people started believing her. Today she is a partner in one of the Big Four accounting firms. She works with the best brains and believes in leveraging her strong network for the betterment of society.

Top 3 Life skill choices – Be consistently progressive, Connecting the dots and Creative Thinking.

Message to Millennials – *She is a firm believer in the 10k-hour rule. Every professional who consistently works hard with sincerity, discipline and dares to chase their dreams despite all the odds will definitely have a "Great Career".*

Anuj Jagannathan (Sr. Director Finance, Visa and Author)

He is a seasoned professional with more than two decades of experience in companies like **Google, Xansa, PwC, Visa and KPMG**. He is a Chartered Accountant, MBA, CPA and holds a certification in Negotiation. His mantra of success has been a firm belief in his abilities and conscious efforts to up-skill (both in the core area as well as adjacencies). He had an opportunity to work in four countries and experience different leadership styles.

With a firm belief in the quote from Warren Buffet - "The people who are most successful are those who are doing what they love", he started working on his passion and authored the book "Negotiation Quotient". He is also a corporate trainer in the field of negotiation.

Life Motto - "I believe in helping you to start believing in yourself."

Top 3 Life skill choices – Challenge the Status Quo, Be Consistently Progressive and Creative Thinking.

***Message to Millennials** – His advice to all Millennials is to focus on continuous learning to meet the challenges of the corporate world. This will propel you to self-growth and build a great career.*

Radha Abrol (Managing Director Accenture)

Her experience spans more than 2 decades at senior positions with companies including **Coca-Cola, Microsoft, American Express and Accenture.**

She stands for Integrity, Compassion, Courage and Commitment. A quote that she stands by - When the Great Scorer comes to write against your name, He writes not that you won or lost but how you played the game!

Top 3 Life skill choices - Challenge the Status Quo, Connecting the Dots and Resist Temptations.

Message to Millennials – 3 core values that every millennial should have are – Integrity, Respect and Perseverance with a strong realization that there is no substitute for hard work.

Veena Sinha (Head Information Services, Culture Change & Corporate Wellness)

Her experience spans more than 3 decades at senior positions with companies including **Steria, Xansa and British Council.**

She started her career as the only female engineer within a setup of 1000+ male engineers in a company situated in a small town in Bihar. Despite several challenges, her self-confidence, gratitude towards family, belief in God and a strong value system (integrity, courage and independence) kept her moving up the corporate ladder. She is also a **"Happiness Coach".**

Top 3 Life skill choices – Celebrate Failure, Challenge the Status Quo and Creative Thinking.

Message to Millennials – The times are tough and excellence is the way forward. Her advice is to develop your USP through "Active Experimentation". It is important to spare some time to pursue your passion as well.

Dr. Major Rupinder Kaur (Leadership Researcher and Coach)

She started her career in the Indian Army and later transitioned into the corporate world before taking a plunge to be a soloprenuer early this year. Her insatiable urge to learn and an appetite for failure facilitated her career transitions. During the entire process of personal change management, she realised – "You will always feel the anxiety when you are moving away from what is familiar. The trick is to tell your mind that this anxiety is unveiling your growth."

A firm believer in the quote from Whitney Houston – **"The only way to reinvent yourself is to disrupt yourself."**

She truly believes in – Being Authentic, Being Empathetic and Giving first, taking later.

Top 3 Life skill choices - Challenge the Status Quo, Imagine to Re-Imagine and Connecting the Dots.

Message to Millennials *– Be like the caterpillar who takes enough time to break the cocoon and when it breaks, nobody can catch the flight. Spend enough time in preparing and once you are ready, do not lead the* *voices of the world stop you from what you want to achieve.*

Aseem Bajaj (Tax Director at Smith & Nephew plc. UK)

With an experience of more than 2 decades spanning India, UK, US and Europe in virtual and real teams, he believes that the most important trait of a thorough professional is about being part of and contributing as a team.

He is an embodiment of trust, reliability, a solution-oriented mindset and excellent work ethics. Despite setbacks, he worked hard and stuck to the value system that defines him as a professional. He believes in mentoring and inspiring co-workers by sharing insights and seeing them succeed.

Top 3 Life skill choices – Challenge the status quo, Connecting the Dots and Resist Temptations and plan for the long term.

Message to Millennials – *Constantly look to upskill, work hard and a clear ability to demonstrate value addition.*

Christoph Steinlen (Partner EY Germany)

Being in the profession for over 14 years now, as he looks back, he realises that it all happened much more quickly than expected. Of course, in the beginning, it was the other way around – nothing happened quickly. He would ruminate over what he was doing wrong, why was nobody noticing his work, etc. This is absolutely natural and is applicable to everyone. The only thing which does not help is giving up too fast and going somewhere else. Perseverance to achieve his goal got him to his destination - Equity Partner in a Big 4 firm.

His 3-pronged strategy included (1) Build your brand on reliability and quality, (2) Being in the right place at the right time is important and (3) Build long term relationships, stand with your team and clients through the thick and thin of things.

Top 3 Life skill choices – Your vision will be your guiding light, resist temptations, plan for the long-term and Creative Thinking – Sometimes a change in the perspective is all that is required.

Message to Millennials – *I have seen a lot of young professionals worry too much at the beginning of the career. If you are in the right firm, deliver on your promises and show a lot of talent to the right people, you* *will eventually come on the right track. Do not get side-tracked by comparing yourselves too much with others – rather invest this time on focusing on yourself and what you can achieve. The thing you might have learned about others is most likely not the whole picture and thus will create an unrealistic picture for you.*

Praises & Recommendations

Akhil and I went to high school together, where he was the Vice Head Boy and I was the Vice Head Girl! It was very long ago... I remember him as a sincere student who loved playing sports all day long. Who knew we would get back in touch again, after so many years, and across continents, to collaborate on this project – **Debotri Dhar (Ph.D., Author of several books, Core Faculty at University of Michigan, Ann Arbor)**

Akhil is a hardworking professional with a hunger to learn and grow. During his corporate journey, he demonstrated high cadence of accountability, had a pleasing personality and was always willing to walk the extra mile to help peers and colleagues – **Charu Mittal (Director Finance, Korn Ferry)**

I remember Akhil as an extremely intelligent and dependable professional. "Your positivity was infectious, and you taught me a lot as I came to a completely new industry. Your work was error-free and that made you stand out as well." He is a wonderful human being, a people's person and a brilliant professional – **Radha Abrol (Managing Director, Accenture)**

What I love about Akhil is his selfless nature which drives him to work for the betterment of people. He is soft at heart and a straight forward person who believes in doing things with utmost sincerity and with the right intention every time – **Kshama Dhir (Partner, EY GDS TAS)**

I had a good rapport with Akhil. Akhil proved very early that he is very reliable and I ensured that he went on to lead independent projects with little oversight from me. He is a strong team player with excellent work ethics that inspire teams to execute consistently – **Aseem Bajaj (Tax Director at Smith & Nephew Plc.)**

It has been a pleasure knowing and interacting with Akhil Iyer. His selfless attitude of reaching out and helping others is remarkable. He has a natural flair for writing, and I wish him all the very best – **Bhuvana Rajaram (Head Content Strategy, Tripura Multinational Pvt Ltd)**

He understands the needs of his team and is always available for them. He built excellent professional relationships with internal and external stakeholders which helped the business to grow at a fast pace – **Amol Sumrani (Associate Director & Regional Head – Fitch)**

He is one of those leaders who live by the fundamentals of being adaptive and flexible at all times. He always puts his heart and soul in all the roles he has handled till date, be it an Operations Leader or donning the hat of a Coach/Mentor – **Kapil Wahal (Head Training & Development and Talent Transformation)**

I believe Akhil has a virtuous mindset for his work and life. He believes in growing and adding value. He is also enterprising and wants to continuously do better things. This shows his growth mindset – **Anuj Jagannathan (Sr. Director Finance, Visa and Author)**

This is an engaging and compassionate book orchestrated by Akhil. The way Akhil has blended his message with his real-life experiences is truly praise-worthy. While reading the book, I found myself getting transported to his shared memoirs. This not only made me relish the spell of reading but also remember the message alloyed to a specific incident. I must say Akhil is a marvelous story-teller.

One of the best attributes is that the book has been written in a simplistic language; you do not need to keep an Oxford handy. Every single mechanism shared by Akhil has great relevance in life which most of us have been missing on. Hence, we often find ourselves fallen between the cracks. Another highlight of the book is the 'Lessons Learnt' at the end of every chapter. After I have read the complete book, I can simply refer to the "Lessons Learnt' for a quick reference.

The book is not like a wall of text with bottomless chapters. Akhil has inked every chapter precisely and meticulously. I read this complete book over the weekend. I highly recommend this book if you are looking to spiral Up the Ladder of life. – ***Sushmitha Naroor Project Manager HSP***

There are very few books that have an emotional connect and this one, born of personal reflections, certainly has. The book completely shatters the myth 'once a winner, always a winner' and 'once a loser, always a loser'. No! Akhil wonderfully quotes 'From an Assistant Director to Mr. Nobody', 'From a handsome six-figure salary to surviving on minuscule savings'. De facto, one victory may not be final; you may have to sometimes lose to discover the greatest pinnacles of life. Where most books speak volumes about success, how to succeed, keys to success, etc., Akhil, with his distilled mindfulness, talks about *'Celebrating Failure'* (which is also one of my favorite chapters). Aaah, who celebrates failure? But after reading this chapter, I do now! This book shines the torch on how to deal with failure and use it as a gateway to growth and transformation.

Many times while reading the appetizing words of wisdom, you may find your eyes steady and unblinking in your face and at times, you may find a smile sliding up your face and settling in. There could be several instances wherein you might stop reading and rather reflect upon what you just read. *(But don't worry if you find yourself enveloped in either of the modes. This is an organic effect of the book.)* Overall, well-thought and perfectly blueprinted!

I recommend this book alias the practical guide to anyone and everyone aspiring for crowning achievements in life. – ***Nitin Dutta Editor, Creative Content Writer***

Akhil joined Author Success Academy a few months back. His zestfulness and commitment to this book were evident in the very first session. Rather I have seen these attributes snowballing not only during our further interactions but they also reflect distinctly in the book. What gives this book an edge is a modernistic approach shared by Akhil using his storytelling skills.

Of course, the rules of the career success game have changed. What used to work a decade back may not be relevant in today's era. This is what makes this book a worth-read for the millennials. They can use this book as a yardstick to make strides Up The Ladder. Besides, in my opinion, not just millennials, but even the senior management people who are working with millennials can gain a basketful of insights from this book. This book mirrors the mindset of the current generation.

I wish Akhil all the best in his endeavors! – *Jyotsna Ramchandran, Founder-Author Success Academy*

Foreword by
Dr. Debotri Dhar

When Akhil asked me to write the foreword for this book, I found it to be a very engaging opportunity to motivate and inspire millennials towards creating self-actualized professional lives. I have always considered my work to be more than just a career – my work is my vocation, my passion, and has allowed me to craft a life for myself that I thoroughly enjoy and feel fulfilled by every day. I would very much like the young millennials to experience that same joy and sense of accomplishment.

The advice that the book has for millennials – the importance of having a vision, planning, celebrating failure, challenging the status quo, creative thinking, and imagining to re-imagine may sound deceptively simple. However, all these are the key to empowered choices and career growth. "Failure", for instance, can not only be the soil in which the seeds of future growth are planted but in many cases a blessing in disguise. I want to share three examples from my own journey.

Gender equality has always been a passion for me; after I completed my Masters from Oxford University with distinction, one field-specific job that materialized immediately was at a social development organisation in rural India. Many saw it as a failure, and as an urban girl, I too found it hard navigating through a forest full of snakes, not to mention a host of other challenges. Yet those months taught me more about pressing gender and developmental issues in rural India than any textbook might. It also allowed me to be closer to my ailing grandfather (though he would joke that a plane from London to Kolkata took as long as the night train from Orissa!). During that time, I put together my Ph.D. applications, took GRE exams, and was accepted with full scholarships in doctoral programs at several top-ranking American universities. After my beloved grandfather passed away, I came to the United States – the university even paid for my flight tickets - and I was able to do my dream work as a scholar and educator in the field of Women's and Gender Studies.

My other two examples are about creative writing, my other passion. I do not hold formal degrees in Literature or creative writing, nor did I know any famous writers to help me as I started my journey. In those days, I had written a long story on Radha, but I could not find a suitable publisher. So, I held on to it, and kept trying to perfect my writing craft on my own alongside my "main" academic work. While on the East Coast, I saved up from my doctoral stipends to attend writing workshops in New York; I remember how I would take the NJ transit, sometimes dozing off because I was so tired from my research and teaching. But I persisted. Some years later, I, not only published several books as a writer and an editor, but my original story on Radha was also published in a beautiful Penguin Random House anthology. Unlike well-connected writers, though, there are seldom invitations to literary festivals, so in 2017, I decided to find my own traveling writers' circle which would create a place not just for me but for other writers as well. This has been a modest success, allowing me to forge literary communities across many states in the United States – New York, California, Oregon, Michigan, Wisconsin, Texas, Vermont - and still counting. In fact, the *Hindustan Times* invited me to write a piece about it, which was published and appreciated in India. Once the pandemic situation improves, I want to take my writers' circle to other countries.

So have faith, keep working hard, think creatively and out of the box, develop resilience practices, know what you are good at, and don't give up easily. Be open to positive criticism and new learning – but also be mindful that not all criticism is either positive or well-meaning or even relevant, so feel free to walk away when necessary. (It is common to speak of the challenges of failure, but success also comes with its own share of challenges!) Finally, do remember that success is not always only up to an individual. There are historical and social injustices, poverty and deprivation, unequal distribution of opportunities and privileges, not to mention personality traits and perhaps some role of luck too. Keeping this in mind allows us to do our own part – the part we have control over - while also having empathy and grace towards the less fortunate, doing what we can for our communities too and not just for ourselves.

In making ourselves, we also make the world – so I hope you make a world that is truly worth living in, for your generation and those to come. Wishing you all the best in your journeys!

Ann Arbor, Michigan, 2020

Thank You !

Thank You For Reading My Book!

I really appreciate all of your feedback and I love hearing what you have to say.

I need your input to make the next version of this book and my future books even better.

Please leave me a helpful review on Amazon letting me know what you thought of the book.

Thank you so much!
Akhil Iyer

www.ingramcontent.com/pod-product-compliance
Lightning Source LLC
Chambersburg PA
CBHW061539120726
48001CB00004B/1636